Scottish
Cycle Routes

Alasdair Cain

30 routes
*South-west, Borders, Central, Perthshire,
Deeside & Speyside,
Inverness & Moray Coast,
West & North-west Coast*

Contents

Published by Mica Publishing 2015
Reprinted 2017

Text and photographs
© Alasdair Cain 2015

Contains Ordnance Survey data © Crown copyright and database right 2015

ISBN 978-0-9560367-7-3

Title page: Around Ben Rinnes, Deeside & Speyside

Maps & design: Mica Publishing
www.micapublishing.com

Printed and bound in India
by Replika Press Pvt Ltd

Mica walkers' guides are distributed by Cordee Ltd; info@cordee.co.uk, www.cordee.co.uk

Disclaimer: While every effort has been made to ensure the accuracy of this guidebook, we accept no responsibility for any loss, injury or inconvenience sustained by anyone using this guide.

3

Scottish Cycle Routes

Near Schiehallion on The Two Lochs route, Southern Perthshire

Welcome to this pocket guide to great road cycling routes in Scotland. Whether an occasional visitor or a resident of the area, hopefully this guide will inspire you to go out there and enjoy the Scottish countryside on two wheels.

During the last few years road biking has taken off in terms of participation numbers. The success of the Olympians and British road bikers such as Nicole Cooke and 'Sir Brad' has brought the sport into the mainstream. The creation of cycle friendly routes and the Sustrans National Cycle Network has encouraged people to 'get on their bikes'. Thousands of riders are attracted to the plethora of sportive events that are all over the country. When I first started cycling in Perthshire you were lucky if you saw one other cyclist even at the weekend. Now, even mid-week, you are more than likely to meet other cyclists.

I originally got 'into' road cycling, firstly to keep fit and then as rehabilitation from a knee operation. Then it became a bit of an obsession. Looking through the bookshelves to get inspiration I was disappointed, there are few books just on road circuits. Most are geared towards cycle touring or a mixture of road and off-road. So I got a map and let my imagination and a bit of research do the rest. As a result I have discovered parts of Scotland I never knew existed. So here are some of the circuits that I think are the best in Scotland – enjoy.

Routes

These are generally on small quiet roads. Sometimes there is no option but to venture onto busier roads and I suggest possible alternatives. Quite a few of the

'It is by riding a bicycle that you learn the contours of a country best, since you have to sweat up the hills and coast down them... you have no such accurate remembrance of country you have driven through.'

Ernest Hemingway

routes do go on main roads, however we are lucky in rural Scotland as most are pretty quiet. I have also used sections of the National Cycle Network, what most cyclists refer to as Sustrans Routes. These extend all over the UK and are very useful for navigating through urban areas and connecting sections of quiet rural roads.

Toilets and the ever important café are mentioned in the text. All of the routes are circular (except one) which reduces the logistical aspect of doing any of the routes. There is the odd 'out and back' section but this will generally be an extension to a circular route. As the weather is not always perfect I have mentioned variations on routes that would be friendlier given adverse conditions. Some routes will cover the same stretches of road and I make no apology for this as these 'duplications' will be worth doing several times anyway.

Route Symbols

▬▬▬	Primary Route
▬▬▬	Extension or Variation
5	Route Number
BRODICK	Start &/or Finish

GWR - Great Wee Road

In the descriptions you will come across the initials GWR from time to time. This terminology has been borrowed from *Raw Spirit* by Iain Banks, a book about travelling round Scotland's whisky distilleries. As he is travelling by car his definition is slightly (!) different from mine. A GWR for me is a road that is quiet, most of the time, and constantly changing, with spectacular views, flowing curves, sudden dips and challenging hills. And when you reach the end you are tempted to go and do it again – almost!

Navigation

For each route I've given distance, height gain, maximum gradient and approximate time at what I think is an average pace. This does not include café stops, sunbathing etc. I have described the routes by using the road numbers, or if a minor road, a description of where that road goes in relation to the numbered roads. All the routes in this guidebook are accompanied by 1:250k Ordnance Survey mapping and you should be able to follow the route, just by reading the description in the book and following the map on the page.

I know a lot of people will be using GPS routes downloaded from a computer. In the last year I have succumbed to this technology and use a Garmin 200 which works well. As long as the route is put in properly! Tracing the map out on whichever programme you use is also good practice as it helps you to familiarise yourself with the route beforehand.

However, technology does break down and batteries go flat, so a map is still worth carrying. The maps in this guidebook should be sufficient, but if you want something lighter then buy a cheap road atlas, they are mostly at the same 1:250k scale, remove the page, transfer your route and put it in an A5 map case or a re-sealable plastic bag.

One word of caution with the use of some of the mapping programmes; the height data given in the properties

The ruins of Ruthven Barracks on Round the Strath, Deeside & Speyside

section is not always accurate. I wrote to one of the main mapping companies in regard to this matter and was informed that this is due to the resolution of the height grid. A high resolution grid would make the product very expensive.

Height Gain

Height gain has been calculated in a number of ways: using the log function on an altimeter; uploading the information from the Garmin; and/or using the profile from mapping programmes and adding together all the up bits! The latter is a laborious process but pretty accurate. Remember to enable the elevation correction on your GPS to get a realistic representation of your height gain. All these methods usually arrive at about the same figure give or take 100m.

The graphs which accompany each route indicate the position of uphill and downhill sections over the course of the route and the spread of total height gain.

Equipment

All the routes have been done on an unladen road bike. The gearing I use on these routes is either a triple chain ring (52-42-30) with a 12-25 cassette or a compact (50-34) with a 12-27 cassette. So you can tell I'm no strongman. Either should get you up any of the hills in the book, with maybe the odd bit out of the saddle. Nowadays you can alter gearing quite easily and fitting ever larger rings on the rear cassette is usually not a problem. If you are unused to hilly terrain it's probably best you try a few short circuits first, before venturing onto the bigger or steeper ones. Most of the routes are 80km/50 miles or more. Options for shorter (or longer!) circuits are mentioned in the text.

Having your bike properly maintained lowers the chance of things going klunk when they are not supposed to. I always carry two spare tubes, tyre levers, a few Allen keys, chain splitter and a few chain links, electrical ties and an old section of toothpaste tube (good for putting in your tyre if you find it's starting to wear through), all packed into an under-seat bag.

This may sound over the top, but over the years I have used all of the above (although not at the same time!). I carry a small pump in one of my rear pockets. In addition to this kit, you need to know how to use it. So if you are unsure, attend a bike maintenance class or get a more knowledgeable person to teach you the basics.

Clothing is another factor to get right, especially in the variable Scottish climate. Always try and carry a water-proof, and have enough layers to keep warm if you have to stop for an extended period.

Food & Water

This is a very personal thing and there is a heap of information in the cycling magazines on this subject. Get it wrong and the ride becomes a nightmare of a struggle. So good preparation is the key. Being fit enough to tackle the ride is the most important criteria and the one most commonly ignored. Eating well and being properly hydrated prior to the ride can make all the difference.

I always carry two 500ml water bottles with an energy powder dissolved in them and a couple of energy bars. This will usually do me for about 3hrs, so long as it's not on the warm side. On much longer runs access to water and food becomes more important hence cafés, public toilets and shops are frequently mentioned in the text. Be aware though, that these facilities might be closed. I have often resorted to asking people in their gardens to fill my water bottle and I also carry a couple of the sport drink powertabs for those refills.

Breakdowns & Emergencies

I am often asked, 'What do you do if you have a major mechanical?' If you are in the area with non-cycling friends you can always contact them, with the fully charged mobile you always carry(!).

However, if you are on your own it changes things considerably. I have always found the general public much more helpful than you think they are going to be. On one occasion I asked at a house if I could leave my precious bike there while I hitched back to get my car, only to be offered a lift back to my car! So help is usually forthcoming. If all else fails remember to carry a bit of cash and/or credit card as using a taxi may be the only solution, but one which I have never had to resort to. As quite a few of the routes in this book are remote, help may take a bit longer to come.

It is good practise to let someone know where you are going and worth carrying some form of identification, so your next of kin can be contacted in the unfortunate event of an accident.

South-west

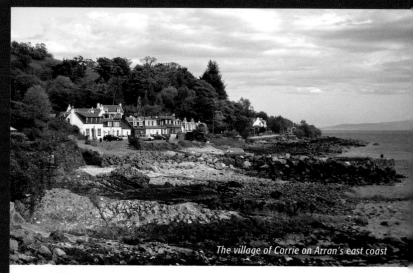

The village of Corrie on Arran's east coast

*G*enerally quiet roads are a feature of this 'forgotten' corner of Scotland, the only busy ones being the A75 and A77 going to and from Stranraer, and the M74 on the eastern boundary.

The area's association with cycling goes way back into the mists of time to local lad Kirkpatrick Macmillan who 'invented' the bicycle back in 1838. A copy of Macmillan's machine can be seen at Drumlanrig Castle's cycling museum, part of **Through the Lowthers** [3].

Another local cycling legend and bike design innovator is Graeme Obree, the 'Flying Scotsman' (check out the book and film), who trains and lives in the north of this area. He is still very active today with some radical bike designs and heroic challenges.

The routes in this chapter take in this under populated hinterland and also the scenic coastal roads from the Solway Firth and the Machars of the Whithorn Peninsula, on up the Ayrshire coast of the Firth of Clyde past 'Paddy's Milestone' (Ailsa Craig) to the magnificent Isle of Arran.

This is a region of wide open views interspersed with thick forest, lonely bleak moors and some stunning coastal scenery. At its centre is the Galloway Forest Park which has recently been designated Europe's Dark Sky Park due to the lack of light pollution. The park

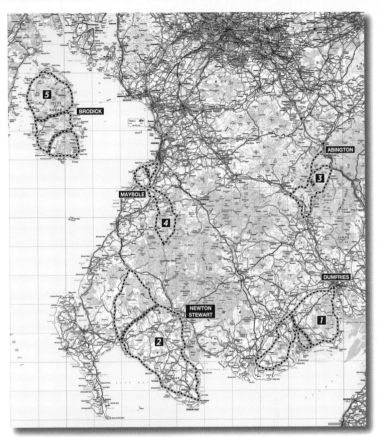

has a visitor centre at Glentrool, which is also home to a 7stanes mountain bike centre, one of four in this part of Scotland.

Professional bike races such as The Tour Doon Hame were staged in the area every Easter up until 2012 and became the stepping stone for many of todays' better known professionals, such as Mark Cavendish. Sadly this race has fallen by the wayside. Recently, Dumfries and Drumlanrig have both hosted stage finishes of the Tour of Britain.

Solway Coast

A scenic coastal tour from historic Dumfries

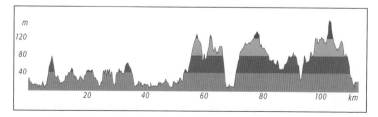

The winding streets of New Abbey

Round the Solway Coast and through the 'milking parlour' of South-west Scotland, this is a scenic route which isn't that hilly, but definitely feels rolling. Much of it is based on the Solway Sportive which takes place in May and parts of the route have also been used in the Tour of Britain.

A good place to start is down by the River Nith in lovely Dumfries. Approaching from the A75 follow the signs for the A710 Solway Coast and Royal Infirmary. At the traffic lights, just before you cross over the River Nith, there is a signposted free car park on your left at the entrance to Dock Park. If approaching from the A701, this car park lies at the south end of White Sands, the road on the north side of

the River Nith. White Sands also has a large car park and public toilets.

Head west out of town over the River Nith to reach the A710 Solway Coast Route and follow it south. This 'A' road is never that busy as you pass through lovely villages and acres of green fields. The village of New Abbey, a short distance from Dumfries, could be used as an alternative start point. At the southern end of the village are the ruins of Sweetheart Abbey where you will find parking, toilets and a handy tearoom.

As you head round the coast you'll start to get views over the Solway Firth to the distant fells of the Lake District beyond. The road then gradually turns north and heads to Dalbeattie. Turn left onto the A711 before the town and cross over the Urr Water. Turn left again just after the bridge heading for Kirkcudbright (not said as it's spelt – Kur koobri is the phonetic) on the A745.

Unfortunately this part of the road stays away from the sea, but the higher ground beyond Auchencairn gives some outstanding views to Cumbria, the Isle of Man and the distant hills of

11

Northern Ireland. If you cycle this route in late May, June or July keep your eyes peeled for a large willow man in a field on your right – The Wicker Man. A music festival is held here every July and climaxes with the burning of this giant statue.

The road then descends to the sea and continues north to Kirkcudbright. The town has public toilets and a fine selection of cafés. Turn right in the town centre onto the well-signposted Sustrans Route 7, following the B727 signposted to Gelston. Turn left at the crossroads before the village onto a minor road signposted to Rhonehouse and continue straight on through Mid Kelton to reach a junction with the B736. Turn right and follow the shore of Carlingwark Loch to Castle Douglas.

Beyond the end of the loch, turn right into Queen Street and follow the Sustrans signs to a Shell Garage. From there, don't follow the Sustrans signs which point off left at a car park and small park, but continue straight on to reach a roundabout and take the second exit signposted A75 Dumfries. The road bears round to the right to another roundabout where you go straight on. About 100m further on, take a right turn with a Sustrans Route

MacLellan's Castle, Kirkcudbright

Auchencairn

7 sign and a signpost to Haugh of Urr.

A few more ups and downs lead through agricultural land with wide open vistas. Cross over the B794 at Haugh of Urr and on past Lochrutton Loch. Turn left at a junction with the A711 and keep straight ahead at the roundabout, following signs to Dumfries. Ignore the Sustrans signs at the next roundabout and stick to the Dumfries road.

Turn right at the next junction, signposted A710 Solway Coast and Royal Infirmary, and right again at the next one, following the same signs. Then take the next left, signposted Royal Infirmary and Town Centre and you are now on the road you headed out on. This will take you back to the River Nith and where you started from.

Dalbeattie Variation
If you wish to do a shorter circuit, take the A710 as far as Caulkerbush then go right onto the B793, and follow it for about 10km to a left turn onto a minor road signposted Dalbeattie ½ mile. Take this into the town, turning right where the road forks beyond Dalbeattie Primary School to reach a mini-roundabout. Turn left here to a T-junction in the town centre. Turn right and down High Street to meet the A711 where you turn left. About 500m further on go right onto the B794 to Haugh of Urr where you join Sustrans Route 7 back to Dumfries. From Haugh of Urr, follow the directions given at the end of the main route back to the car park. This is a lovely little route for those wishing less exercise.
Total distance 65km (40 miles); Height gain 450m (1476ft);
Max gradient 15%; Approx time 2hrs 30mins

North over Portyerrock Bay to Cairnsmore of Fleet

orestry, bleak open moor and the Machars coast make this a route of considerable contrast. The route starts in the small town of Newton Stewart on the River Cree and crosses north over the watershed, before heading back south to the coast and historic Isle of Whithorn.

Coming into Newton Stewart from the south on the A714 and just beyond the Bank of Scotland, there is parking and toilets signposted on the right, down by the banks of the River Cree. You'll also find The Belted Galloway Visitor Centre here, which has a lovely café awaiting your return.

Go back to the A714 and follow it north, then turn left onto the B7027, signposted Challoch and Knowe. This very quiet road traverses through a lot of industrial forest plantations with the odd bit of natural woodland. At Loch

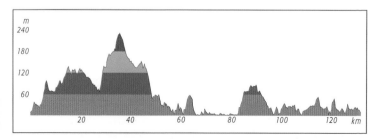

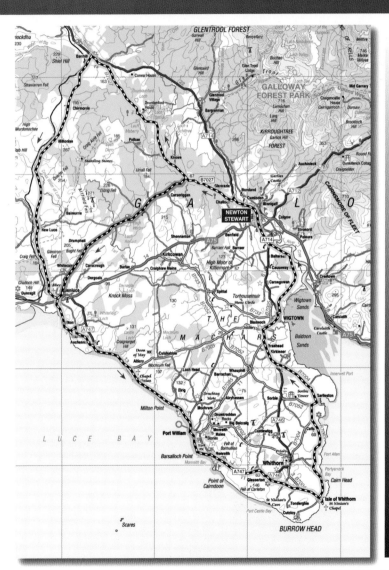

Luce Bay and the Mull of Sinniness

Maberry the plantations give way to open views across the myriad of small lochs before closing in again prior to a final open section leading to a junction with the A714 at Barrhill, where there's a shop but not much else

Turn left back onto the A714 and once through Barrhill, turn left onto a minor road signposted New Luce. The road climbs briefly through more conifer plantations before reaching its highest point where the scenery opens out into bleak moorland as the road starts its long descent. The railway out to your right is the main Glasgow to Stranraer line and runs parallel with the road as far as the village of Glenluce.

The bleak moor gradually gives way to agricultural land, hedgerows and trees as you pass through New Luce, then on past the ruins of Glenluce Abbey and under a railway viaduct to a T-junction. A left turn leads to Glenluce itself which has a shop. Turn right and head down towards the A75, to take a signposted cycleway on your right, just

---

Three Lochs Variation
There are obviously many variations to be made with the road network in the area, but if you feel this route is over long, you can reduce the distance with this variation. Follow the the B7017 north from Newton Stewart as for the main route, then turn left about 2km beyond Spectacle and Garwachie Lochs onto a minor road signposted Glenluce.
Follow this road south-west past Black Loch, Loch Heron and Loch Ronald – the Three Lochs – to arrive at Glenluce. Turn right through the village and join the main route as it drops down to the A75.
Total distance 105km (65 miles); Height gain 480m (1575ft);
Max gradient 15%; Approx time 4hrs 30mins

before the T-junction. This takes you beneath the A75 by a beautifully decorated underpass and on to reach Stairhaven (public toilet) with lovely views over the sands of Luce Bay.

Follow the road round left and up a hill to South Milton farm, then turn right onto a scenic and very skinny single track road which takes you through open fields to a junction with the A747, where you turn right to Port William. The road flattens out as you cycle alongside the sea to the village where you will find a shop but sadly no cafés.

A couple of kilometres further on the road heads inland to Monreith, climbs over the Machars peninsula and continues straight on beyond Glasserton, signposted Isle of Whithorn. It's not an island at all but a village with a pretty harbour where you'll find a friendly wee shop which serves hot drinks and food.

Retrace your tracks back round the harbour and turn right, signposted to Garlieston (B7063). There is a public toilet on the right just after this junc-tion. After the scattered buildings of Portyerrock the road goes inland and you have the odd glimpse of the sea. At the next junction turn right onto the B7063, then right at the next onto the B7004, then right again – all signposted Garlieston. Just before Garlieston, a pretty seaside village, turn left signposted Wigtown and remain on the B7004 to a junction with the A746, where you turn right to Wigtown. The town is Scotland's national book town and home to a major annual book festival in the autumn.

Entering Wigtown turn right and head along the main street, ignoring all turnings, to where the road becomes narrower. Descend past the war memorial and trend left round Wigtown Sands at the estuary of the River Cree. Continue along this minor road, going straight on at any junctions, to reach the River Cree and the junction with the A714 near St Ninian's Well. Here you turn right to a roundabout and continue straight ahead back into Newton Stewart.

Isle of Whithorn harbour

Wanlockhead – highest village in Scotland

*V*iewed from the M74 to the east, the Lowther Hills can look rather bleak, but the western flanks have some lovely glens with quiet roads winding through them. The sense of desolation is magnified by the various abandoned mine workings, particulary around Wanlockhead (the highest village in Scotland) where there is a lead mining museum and steam railway. Fortunately the Lowthers are not yet covered in wind turbines, unlike the hills around Beattock and Abington.

This route starts from Abington village beside the M74 and is one of the best combinations of roads in the area. Start from the car park beside the Bank of Scotland on the east side of the A702 at the south end of the village. Unfortunately, the toilets are often locked.

From the car park, go left out of the

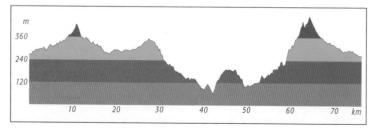

village on the A702, then right onto the B797, signposted to Leadhills. After the gradual climb to Leadhills take a sharp left onto the B7040 to Elvanfoot. Enjoy the gradual descent to a right turn onto the A702 and follow this alongside the River Clyde, before turning towards the hills and a gradual climb to the head of the Dalveen Pass, followed by a lovely sweeping descent through impressive mountain scenery.

As you descend into Nithsdale you go under a railway bridge and about 1km further on take a right onto a minor road signposted Drumlanrig Castle. At the A76 turn right then immediately left (Drumlanrig) and follow the minor road down and round to the left, then over the River Nith to a junction where you take a right. The now red coloured road climbs gradually up into the grounds of the estate to become a tree-lined avenue leading to the castle car park and entrance.

The castle has a café if you are in need of refreshment and there are also various mountain bike trails, a cycling museum (Kirkpatrick Macmillan who 'invented' the bicycle in 1838 lived

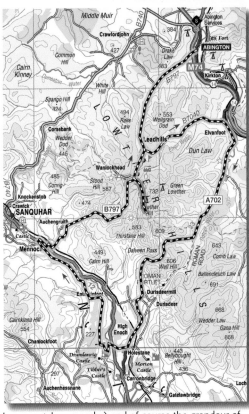

nearby) and of course the grandeur of a tour of 'the hoose' itself.

If a castle visit isn't in the itinerary then turn right off the red road onto a black one with a cycle route sign, which ascends towards Drumlanrig Mains farm.

Ascend past the farm and continue north on the black road which climbs away from the River Nith and provides a great viewing balcony overlooking

The Mennock Pass

Nithsdale and the Lowther Hills beyond. After 5km you reach a T-junction where you turn right and descend to a bridge over the River Nith. Don't cross over, but turn left just before the bridge keeping to the west bank of the River Nith for about 4km, to reach another bridge and a junction with the A76.

Turn right and go through the hamlet of Mennock to a left turn onto the B797, signposted to Wanlockhead and Abington. This is the start of the climb to the Mennock Pass which is fairly steady at first but flattens out in its middle section, where it is worth keeping an eye out for people panning for gold in the river. As the hills close in, the road steepens up for the last 5km to the pass.

Whizz past Wanlockhead and be prepared for a little more up, the sting in the tail, before descending through Leadhills and back to Abington.

Lowther Hill Extension

If you are of a masochistic bent and want to keep climbing after reaching Wanlockhead – you can. At the very northern end of the village, on the east side of the B797, a small road turns off right to a blue doored garage building above the road.

This private, very well surfaced road is owned by National Air Traffic Services and leads to the summit of Lowther Hill. You will need to dismount to get over the barrier at the start and the steepest bit is at the end. The wind may make it even harder! Have fun. I would thoroughly recommend it as the views are outstanding. The Mont Ventoux of Scotland?

Distance 4km (2.5 miles); Height gain 350m (1148ft); Max gradient 17%;

4

Burns Country
From rural Ayrshire to the Galloway hills

Isle of Arran from near Dunure

Centred round the town of Maybole, south of Ayr, this figure of eight route is mainly on very quiet roads and includes three of the area's iconic climbs; some of the Ayrshire Alps. The area is also the home of two famous Scotsmen, the celebrated poet Robert Burns who spent his early life in this area, and Graeme Obree, cycling's 'Flying Scotsman' who continues to use many of the roads for training.

Travelling south on the busy A77 to Stranraer, there is a car park with toilets on the left at the south end of Maybole, beyond the town hall and clock tower. From the car park, go left onto the main street and take the second left onto a minor road marked as Sustrans Route 7 and signposted to Dailly and Kilkerran. Pass Auchenwynd and go under the railway to a left turn onto a minor road with a Sustrans sign. Pass over the railway and continue to a T-junction with the B7023 and make a right turn to Crosshill.

Go through Crosshill, signposted Straiton and Dalmellington, to reach

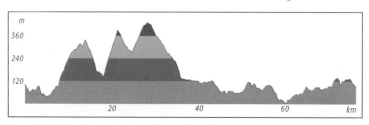

the B741 and cross over, signposted Glentrool and Newton Stewart. The route now ascends through agricultural land to forestry plantations and open moorland on a well-surfaced single track road which is never steep but fairly relentless. After crossing Black Hill of Garleffin, 5km of twisty descent takes you to North Balloch where you keep following the Sustrans signs.

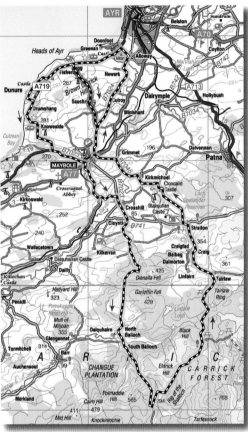

You now start the scenic climb to the Nick o' the Balloch. The road surface is good, as is the gradient; steady but never steep. After passing through the Nick and over the side of Rowantree Hill there is a short descent to a road junction where you take a left, signposted to Straiton and Ayr. Just after the junction, at Rowantree Bridge, there is a memorial to David Bell (1907-1965), who wrote articles on cycling under the *nom de plume* The Highwayman and had a weekly column in the *Ayrshire Post*.

Another steady climb takes you over the windswept northern ridge of Shalloch on Minnoch (433m) to Stinchar Bridge, followed by a lovely sweeping descent to Tairlaw Bridge over the Water of Girvan, then north to the village of Straiton.

Go down Main Street following signs for B7045, Ayr and Kirkmichael. At the end of Main Street there is a public toilet and also a café and shop if you are in need of sustenance. Continue down past the church, ignore the turning on the left to Maybole, and continue to Kirkmichael. Some 2.5km out of Kirkmichael on the B7045, turn left onto a minor road signposted Maybole and follow this to meet the A77 at the north end of the town.

Turn left and follow the main street to the first turning on the right; Redbrae. (If you want to return to the start, then follow the main street back to the car park). Ascend Redbrae sharply round left to a T-junction with Barns Terrace and turn right onto the B7024, signposted Alloway.

Follow this road all the way to the famous Brig o' Doon in Alloway, which is easily viewed from the road bridge across the River Doon. This was the bridge over which Tam O'Shanter escaped from Nannie the witch in the final verse of Robert Burns' famous poem. Continue for about 650m to just before the Burns Cottage and turn left, onto Greenfield Avenue, signposted (A719) Turnberry and follow it to a junction with the A719. Here the route turns left onto the A719 and follows it towards Dunure, but a short variation is also possible along the coast.

For this variation, cross straight over and down the lane to the right of the

Ascending the Nick o' the Balloch

Spar shop. This becomes a cycle path beside the River Doon, which is then crossed via the Millennium Bridge near its mouth. Continue along the cycle path beyond to a small car park on the sea front. Gain the residential coast road and follow it right to a cycle path link to a road giving access to a larger car park, a good alternative starting point for the route.

Turn left to the road and follow it past the houses to where a tarmac route branches off right past Greenan, then left past High Greenan. Follow the access road to a cycle path on the right leading to the A719. Continue west on the A719, ignoring the left turn for Sustrans Route 7 and Carrick Hills. This is the Brown Carrick Hill Variation described opposite.

The road now climbs gradually round the coast to where a short detour off to the right can be made through the village of Dunure. This gives great views over the small harbour and ruins of Dunure Castle to Arran and the Mull of Kintyre beyond.

Further along the A719, the distinctive mound of Ailsa Craig appears to

Brig o' Doon, Alloway

the south-west as you traverse the phenomenon of the 'Electric Brae'. This slope provides an optical illusion making it look as if the slope is going the other way. Therefore, a stationary car on the road with the brakes off will appear to move slowly uphill. The term 'Electric Brae' dates from a time when it was incorrectly thought to be a phenomenon caused by electric or magnetic attraction within the Brae.

About 3.5km further on you'll arrive at a T-junction where you turn left onto the B7023 back to Maybole, turning down right to the A77 and the main street. Turn right back to the car park.

Brown Carrick Hill Variation

Rather than going west round the coast from Ayr then south-east to Maybole, a hillier direct alternative can be made over Brown Carrick Hill. From the A719 coast road at the Heads of Ayr, turn left onto a minor road signposted Carrick Hills and Sustrans Route 7.

It is a steep and unrelenting climb, but your reward is outstanding views over Ayr and the Firth of Clyde. For anyone with bags of energy left, then just before the highest point, a tree-lined access road heads off to the right and leads to the summit aerials.

Beyond this high point, make a steady descent south, watching out for stray cattle and sheep on the road. After the sharp left bend at Sauchrie, ignore a right turn signposted Sustrans Route 7, and continue to join the B7024. Turn right and descend to reach Maybole at Barns Terrace, above the railway station. Take the first left into Redbrae and descend to the main street and A77, where a right turn leads back to the car park.

Total Distance 81km (50 miles); Height gain 1040m (3412ft);
Max gradient 20%; Approx time 4hrs

5

Arran Circuit

A taste of the Highlands in the Firth of Clyde

Boarding a Cal Mac ferry to any of Scotland's islands is a special experience, particularly when the sea is like glass and the sun is sparkling in the sky. Arran lies just 19.5km (12 miles) out in the Firth of Clyde and is one of the most accessible islands, but it feels like another world; a much more relaxing one.

It is possible to circumnavigate the island in a day and there is also the added challenge of the island's two celebrated hill climbs; The String and The Ross. The String is the B880 which starts just north of Brodick, climbs to 234m, then descends south to

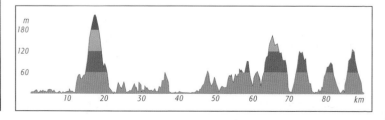

START & FINISH: Car park,
Ardrossan ferry terminal (NS
224419)

DISTANCE: 90km; 56 miles

HEIGHT GAIN: 880m; 2887ft

MAX GRADIENT: 20%

APPROX TIME: 4hrs

Blackwaterfoot and Arran's western peaks

Blackwaterfoot, while The Ross is the minor road which starts from the A841 just south of Lamlash, climbs to 285m, then descends to the coast road between Lagg and Sliddery.

Arran is easily accessed by ferry from the town of Ardrossan, north of Ayr, where there is modestly priced 24hr car parking on your left before the terminal. The island is very cycle friendly and the local council have been pro-active in making road users (whether cars or cycles) aware of their responsibilities to each other.

The route is described in an anti-clockwise direction, but which way you circumnavigate Arran will depend on the current wind direction. If it is blowing from the south-west, then it is best to go clockwise as the west coast is quite exposed, but this does mean you are confronted with getting off the ferry to face the immediate, short, sharp shock of the hill south of Brodick on the A841 to Lamlash.

From Brodick the fairly flat A841 coastal road is followed north through Corrie to the first climb of the day up Glen Sannox. It is a fairly steady ascent through impressive mountain scenery, followed by a lovely descent to Lochranza where you will find toilets, a distillery, cafés and an imposing ruined castle.

The road then turns round the head of the island and snakes south along

Kintyre ferry at Lochranza

the coast which is fairly flat. You are now looking west over Kilbrannan Sound to the Kintyre peninsula. Sandy beaches, palm trees – is this really Scotland? Keep an eye out for seals, herons and if you are really lucky, otters down by the beach.

There's a café at Pirnmill a short distance down the coast and toilets and a shop in Blackwaterfoot right down at the southern end. After Blackwaterfoot the road is quite lumpy all the way back to Brodick. There's a big 'lump' at Kilmory at the southern tip with a steep descent and ascent (20%) to and from the Kilmory Water.

Further east, before the road swings north up the coast, it is worth turning

Kintyre from Arran's west coast

right and taking the steep road (20%) down to Kildonan on the coast, where there is a small shop but not much else. It's a great place for a 'chill' before continuing up the road out of the village (not as steep as the one you came down) back to the main road.

Turn right and continue to Whiting Bay where there are plenty of cafés, then round to Lamlash for fine views east to Holy Island and the final hill of the day, up and over to Brodick.

The String & The Ross Variation

For those wishing a bit more of a full day can vary the route by including The String and The Ross (see main text). Both are more sustained and steeper on their eastern sides, The Ross being the harder of the two. The best combination is probably a figure-of-eight circuit starting from Brodick and going anti-clockwise round the island via Lochranza, then east over The String to Brodick. From there go south to Lamlash, west over The Ross and anti-clockwise back round the south and east coast to Brodick. A great day out.

Total distance 108km (67 miles); Height gain 1430m (4692ft); Max gradient 20%; Approx time 5hrs

The Borders

The roads around Peebles are famous for their cycle races

To the south and east of Edinburgh lie the Borders. From the scenic coastline the area stretches inland through mainly arable farmland to the rolling hills and moors of the Moorfoots and the Lammermuirs. The roads in the area are not that busy, apart from main trunk roads and during the daily commute. Being reasonably close to Edinburgh there are usually quite a few cyclists out and about, especially at the weekend.

The area is home to one of the most popular mountain bike centres at Glentress, just outside Peebles. The town has seen a lot of bike action in recent years. The Tour of Britain has

Start of the Tour of Britain – Peebles

used the town as the starting point for the event on a number of occasions and each May there is something for everyone at the Tweedlove Bike Festival. There is a very active cycle club in the town and they organise the annual Tour of Tweeddale Sportive in September. Does Peebles qualify as 'Cycle Town of Scotand'?

The routes described in this chapter are all relatively close to Edinburgh, although there is obviously much more to explore in the area to the south, towards the Cheviot Hills and over the border into Northumberland.

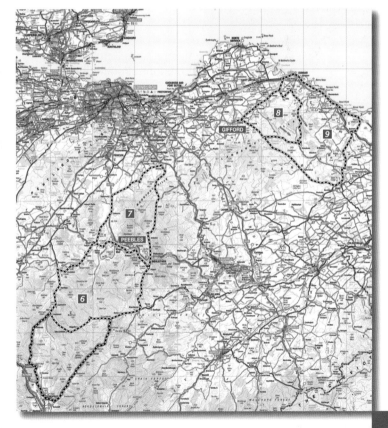

Climbing above Talla Reservoir

*u*sually quiet, main and minor roads are a feature of this circuit through the heart of Borders country, taking in the delight of the steep climb (20%) up to Talla Moss and the Megget Stone.

Cross the Tweed and head west out of Peebles along the A72 above the river past historic Neidpath Castle. This road can be a bit busy, but the traffic eases once you turn left onto the B712 to Broughton. The route now follows the Tweed again and you may notice the markings for the Stobo 10 mile time trial course, which is used for various events throughout the summer. Pass the beautiful botanic garden at Dawyck and the village of Drumelzier,

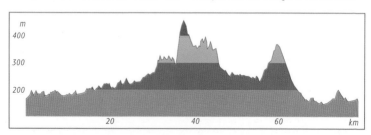

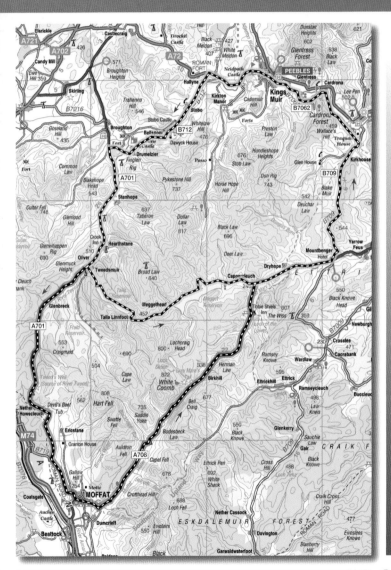

Crossing Talla Moss near the Megget Stone

said to be the burial place of Merlin of Arthurian legend, to reach the A701.

Turn left, signposted to Moffat, and continue past the Crook Inn to Tweedsmuir and a left turn onto a minor road signposted to Talla and Fruid. As you pass through the hills and cycle alongside Talla Reservoir, you will clearly see the road ahead, clawing its way up the side of the hill to Talla Moss and the Megget Stone. It's a short, sharp, shock and gradually lessens in angle as you grovel upward – honest!

Once you've got your breath back and taken in the view, your reward is a great ride down, past Meggett

Reservoir to St Mary's Loch. The road starts off pretty skinny but once along the shores of the reservoir it widens out and with a west wind behind you, you can fairly move along.

At the junction turn left and head along the A708 as far as the Gordon Arms Hotel. Here you turn left onto the B709, locally known as Paddy Slacks, and climb up and over (not too steep) to Traquair.

Just before the village take the B7062 on your left. This follows the south side of the River Tweed, past Cardrona, and over a couple of short hills back to Peebles.

Moffat Extension

If you fancy a longer stretch of the legs you can miss out the steep climb to the Megget Stone and keep on the A701 to Moffat. This is a gradual climb to the top of the scenic and historic Devil's Beef Tub, a deep hollow in the hills where Border Reivers hid their stolen cattle, followed by a gradual descent into the market town of Moffat where there are plenty of cafés. After that you pay the price as you now have another gradual climb back up the scenic Moffat Dale on the A708 passing the Grey Mare's Tail waterfall on your left, then a superb sweeping descent to Loch of the Lowes. At the far end of this, on the left, is the Glen Café; a fine watering hole. Another 3km further on, a minor road sign-posted to Tweedsmuir appears on the left. This is where you rejoin the Megget route. Although the roads you take on this route are main roads, they are rarely that busy.

Total distance 110km (68 miles); Height gain 850m (2789ft);
Max gradient 12%; Approx time 4hr 30min

7 Through the Moorfoots
Riverside & rolling hill roads

From a start in Peebles, this circuit goes through then round the Moorfoot Hills on some quiet roads. The route across the north side is very scenic with lovely views of the Pentland Hills and the distant hills of Fife. The north side of the Moorfoots is high up and relatively treeless so it's exposed to the elements.

Leave the car park and head east on the south side of the River Tweed on the B7062 and Sustrans cycle route past Cardrona to Traquair then Innerleithen. Innerleithen can also be reached by a cycle path on the north side of the River Tweed, accessed from the east end of Peebles High Street; beware of pedestrians!

Once on Innerleithen's main street take a left onto the B709. You are now on Sustrans Route 1 which you follow to the other side of the Moorfoots. This gradually climbs through the hills to Garvald Lodge where you go straight ahead on the B7007, with a lovely scenic descent down the north side of the Moorfoots.

Before reaching the A7 at the bottom of the hill, turn left onto a minor road to Middleton. Turn left at the cross-roads, following the Sustrans cycle route signpost to Bonnyrigg and at the next junction take a left, (the Sustrans route continues northwards), signposted to Outerston, Yorkston and Temple. Go straight on at the next

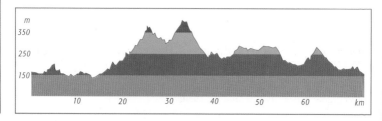

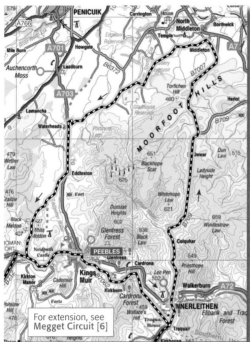

For extension, see
Megget Circuit [6]

left turn, signposted Moorfoot and Peebles. Go straight on at any further junctions and make a short steep (15%) descent to the A703 where you turn left towards Peebles. It's easy to get lost in this area with a plethora of small roads. If in doubt, head west.

The A703 can be busy especially at peak commuting times. There is a café on your left just before Eddleston, The Scots Pine, if you are in need of some sustenance.

In Eddleston take a right, opposite the Horseshoe restaurant, and climb gradually to the high point just before White Meldon (on the left) and Black

junction (Yorkston) and take a left at the next, which goes up a short hill.

Take a right at the next junction, the road ahead is a dead end, and follow the road round Gladhouse Reservoir until you come to a T-junction and a

Meldon (on the right), from where a gradual descent takes you down towards the A72. Lower down, keep left where the road divides, to reach the A72 and follow it left back to Peebles.

Megget Extension – Combining the Two
*A longer route can be made for anyone who is a glutton for punishment. At the junction with the A72 south of White and Black Meldon, take a right then a left onto the road signposted Broughton and Stobo. You are now on the **Megget Circuit [6]** described in the previous route. Follow the directions for this.*
Total distance 120km (74.5 miles); Height gain 1300m (4265ft);
Max gradient 20%; Approx time 5hr 30min

Short but sharp

Crystal Rig windfarm from above Whiteadder Reservoir

South-east of Edinburgh lie the Lammermuir Hills, more a huge area of moorland, than distinctive hills and quite exposed to any extreme weather. This is a shortish but fairly brutal circuit going over Bransley Hill and through Crystal Rig wind farm on some very quiet roads.

The village of Gifford 7km south of Haddington provides the starting point for this route. You'll find plenty of parking and a public toilet down beside the park, which is just beyond the village centre as you enter from Haddington. There's also that all important café for your return.

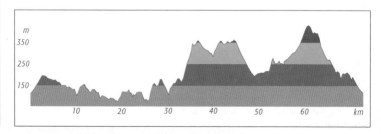

Head out of Gifford on the B6355 signposted to Duns, passing to the right of the church as you exit the village. After about 1.5km, turn left onto the B6370 signposted to Garvald and follow it for 6km to a T-junction, where you turn right, signed to Dunbar. Pass through Stenton and leave the B6370 at Pitcox, taking a right onto a minor road signed to Pathead Farm. The road starts to climb and at the next junction take a left to Spott; the road ahead is signposted Pathead and a dead end.

On reaching Spott turn right, signposted to Brunt, and here the grunt (excuse the pun) really begins. There is a sharp downhill bend and a ford to cross over the Dry Burn! On the other side, after a sharp bend, pass a minor road off left then one off right. Arriving at a T-junction take a right, past Elmscleugh Farm where the road eases for a brief respite.

Now 'gird your loins' as the road climbs steeply up to the moor and eventually eases as you enter the Crystal Rig wind farm. It is worth stopping to get your breath back and take in the view. East Lothian, Berwick Law, Bass Rock (that's the one in the sea) and Fife beyond, are all laid out below you.

The road descends into conifer plantations and although it's unlikely you'll meet a vehicle, you never know, so take care. A short bit of up brings you to a fork in the road. It doesn't matter which fork you take as

they both lead to the B6355 and the Whiteadder Water. Turn right, signposted to Gifford. It is a gradual climb, with a short steep bit at Whiteadder Reservoir, to the summit of the moor and more stunning views looking west towards the Pentland Hills, Edinburgh and the Forth Valley beyond. Then there's a lovely sweeping descent to Gifford which unfortunately has a little dip on the way – just to keep you on your toes!

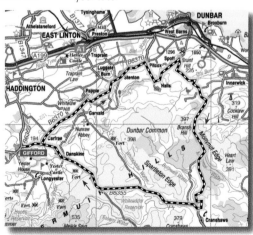

9 Over the Lammermuirs
Sea views & a high moorland crossing

Lothian coast from above Pease Bay

Starting from the flatlands of East Lothian, this route goes round the east coast and over to the border town of Duns, before climbing back over the Lammermuir Hills and takes in some of the area's classic climbs.

Start in the village of Gifford 7km south of Haddington. There's a café for your return, plenty of parking and a public toilet down beside the park, just beyond the village centre as you enter from Haddington.

Head out of Gifford on the B6355 signposted to Duns, passing to the right of the church as you exit the village. About 1.5 km further on, turn left onto the B6370 signposted to Garvald and follow it for 6km to a T-junction and a right turn, signposted to Dunbar. Pass through Stenton and Pitcox towards Dunbar.

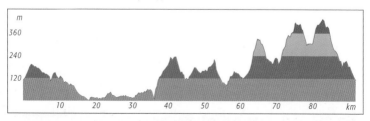

At the junction with the A1, take the third exit from the roundabout past The Store café, a good stopping place. This is a vehicular No Through Road which runs uphill then left over the railway. Out of hours the road is gated, but a cycle path leads beside the eastbound dual carriageway for 200m and then links in with the road. Go straight on through the small housing estate where the road bears left up to a junction with the A1087, where a right turn leads towards the town centre.

This road bears right at a mini roundabout and you cycle along Dunbar's main street heading out of town with

the sea on the left. Continuing on the A1087 you arrive at a roundabout and take the first exit signposted to the cement works which you can see smoking ahead of you. At the layby on the left, take the Sustrans cycle path off left alongside the railway (an unsurfaced path for about 500m) to rejoin the roadway, which comes down from the entrance to the cement works. Cross the railway and take the second of two roads, heading east for Torness Nuclear Power Station.

The route crosses the A1 in front of Torness and continues as a cycle path, then a road past Dunglass, to just

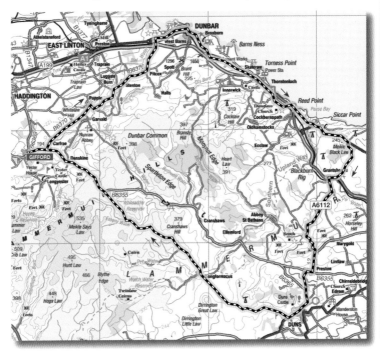

Berwickshire coast

beyond a roundabout on the A1 where an underpass leads beneath the A1 to a road which passes Cove then descends to Pease Bay. This is a sheltered cove, covered in caravans and very popular with surfers. After crossing the ford at the caravan site you start the first iconic climb of the day. The first 2km are the steepest, but the angle relents as height is gained.

Arriving at the junction with the A1107, turn left and keep climbing up to Penmanshiel Moor. Just before the crest of the hill and the wind farm, leave Sustrans Route 76 and take the minor road on the right (Sustrans Route 1). Don't forget to look behind at the great view up the coast to Berwick Law on the left and Bass Rock with Fife behind and of course, Torness Power Station. The road climbs for a short distance before descending to the A1. The surface in places is not the best, however the views more than compensate as the distant Cheviot Hills can be seen away to the south.

Just before the A1 you will come across the Cedar Cafe where you turn right. To avoid the A1 take a walkway on the right to the village of Grantshouse. Back on the road veer left to the A1 and cross over to the A6112,

signposted to Duns. Ignore the Sustrans route off right at the start and follow the road over a couple of hills, then descend to Preston.

The Sustrans loop re-joins just before Duns, where there are cafés and toilets. Continue out of town on the A6195 for 1.5km, ignoring the Sustrans route off left, and take a minor road signposted to Gifford, which climbs past the golf course, never too steeply, but relentlessly, over Hardens Hill. To the south-west lies the Merse, the valley of the River Tweed with the distinctive lumps of the Eildon Hills near Melrose.

After descending to Longformacus past Dirrington Great Law the road winds its way up out of the trees and onto the open moor of Mainslaughter Law. Another descent, then it is upwards again over a wild and exposed bit of road with tired little legs screaming in protest.

All of a sudden you reach the junction with the B6355 and the **Whiteadder Circuit [8]**. The whole of East Lothian is laid out below and to the west, the Pentland Hills, Edinburgh and the Forth Valley beyond. The finale is a lovely sweeping descent to Gifford which unfortunately has a little dip on the way.

*Climbing out of Pease Bay –
spot the surfers*

Central

West over the Tay towards Perth

entral Scotland lies between the Highland Boundary Fault to the north and the Southern Upland Fault to the south and conjures up images of grim towns and cities and a landscape laid waste by heavy industrial activity.

That may have been the case 30 years ago, but today the region is much improved. Many of the towns and cities are a delight to visit and very bike friendly, with well signposted Sustrans cycle routes taking you round or through the conurbations.

The area encompasses a wide variety of scenery, landscape and culture, from the highland landscape surrounding the sea lochs on the west coast, through to the delightful coastline and villages of Fife. Although the bulk of the population live in this region, it is amazing how easily you can get into what feels like remote country.

To the north and west of Glasgow is Scotland's first national park, Loch

Lomond & The Trossachs, which feels very Highland but is within easy reach of the Central Belt. Further to the east the Ochil Hills rise up to the north-east of Stirling, but no roads traverse through them until you reach Glen Eagles and Glen Devon at the eastern end. From here looking over to the east and stretching to the sea is the ancient Kingdom of Fife, which has many nooks and crannies for the road biker to explore.

These circuits are spread across the area and include some urban cycling through two of Scotland's smaller cities and even the use of a lift!

The access road round Loch Katrine

Since the early 1800s the area known as The Trossachs, on the western edge of Central Scotland, has been popular with tourists, mainly due to the literature of Sir Walter Scott.

Loch Katrine, one of the primary water supply reservoirs for Glasgow, lies at the heart of the area and a private access road round its northern shore and western tip can be linked into a fine circuit. The whole route is fairly short but involves a good bit of climbing.

This part of the Loch Lomond & The Trossachs National Park can be very popular in the summer and the best time to visit is spring or autumn when the colours can be breathtaking.

There is a large pay & display car park in Aberfoyle behind the Tourist Information Office and public toilets. Get warmed up as the climbing starts straight away. From Aberfoyle's main street take the road heading north, signposted A821 to Callander. This is the Duke's Pass, named after the Duke of Montrose who constructed a road over the eastern shoulder of Craigmore to join the older road at the entrance to the Pass of Trossachs.

It's up all the way at a fairly steady gradient with a steeper part just after The Lodge Visitor Centre, followed by a

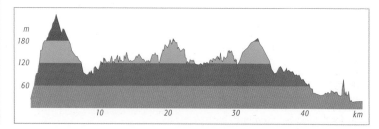

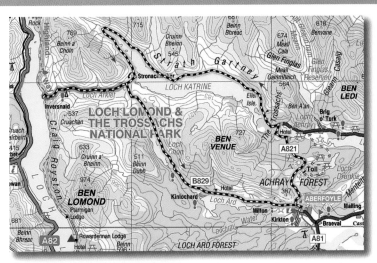

sweeping, scenic descent to the western end of Loch Achray. Turn left, sign-posted Loch Katrine, and go through the Pass of Trossachs to the eastern end of Loch Katrine. Go through the car park and pick up the private road running round the north shore.

Initially there may be quite a few pedestrians and other cyclists, especially for the first few kilometres but after that it is virtually your own private GWR (Great Wee Road). The road rolls round the loch and meets the B829 west of Stronachlachar. There is a nice café down by the pier to the left. Turn left at the junction onto the B829 and it's a roller coaster of a return past Loch Chon and Loch Ard to Aberfoyle.

The route is like a dram of malt whisky. Not a lot of it, but what there is, is real quality.

Inversnaid Extension
A side excursion can be made beside Loch Arklet to the bonnie banks of Loch Lomond at Inversnaid. By far the steepest road of the day will be encountered as you climb back up from the loch. The reward can be a stop at the Inversnaid Bunkhouse café which is at the top of the hill.
Distance 13km (8 miles); Height gain 250m (820ft); Max gradient 20%

Puffing up from Dunning

The Ochils run in a north-easterly direction from Stirling. Most of the roads go round them but there are a few which traverse across. The best place to start is Auchterarder (just off the A9), where there is a car park and toilets on the south side of the high street. The figure of eight circuit described here is not too long, but as you can see from the profile there isn't a lot of flat. Quite a few of these roads are used in the Sportive Kinross which usually takes place in April.

Turn right fom the car park and head east down the high street of the 'lang toon' to open countryside and the B8062, signposted to Dunning. Go through this village passing St Serfs Church on your left, then straight ahead over the Dunning Burn, signposted Newton of Pitcairns and Path of Condie. Hopefully by now your legs are warmed up as the next bit, known as Dragon Hill, is short but brutal.

Local legend tells of St Serf, who slew a dragon with the help of his pastoral staff in Dunning, but the name may also relate to the road profile for this section, which resembles a set of uneven dragon's teeth.

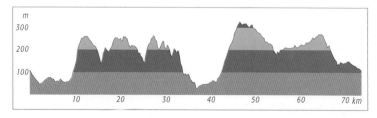

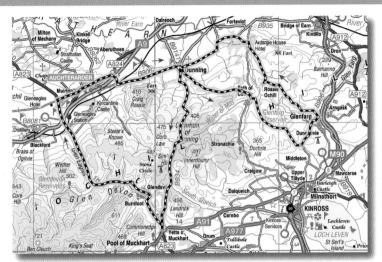

Continue over the high ground and descend to a junction before Pathstruie. Turn right, signposted Glenfarg, make a steep twisty descent to Pathstruie, then cross over the Water of May and keep straight ahead. There's now a climb up and out of the 'dip' of Pathstruie, but fortunately it is a bit shorter and not as steep as the previous ascent. Descend to a T-junction just beyond Newhill Farm and turn left, signposted Glenfarg.

Go left at the T-junction in Glenfarg, then next left into Hayfield Road. This starts climbing just after a right-hand bend to above Glenfarg Reservoir. Once up, there are still a few more lumps before the descent. The Lomond Hills of Fife dominate the skyline behind and to the south.

This road is particularly thin and there is often grit about, so take care on the descent to Ardargie. At the T-junction go right for about 500m, then turn off left – both are signposted to Forteviot.

After a kilometre, turn left at a T-junction signposted to Dunning. Cross over the Water of May and on through agricultural land with wide open views to reach Dunning. Turn right past St Serfs Church, then left onto the B934 to Yetts o' Muckhart. What follows is a delightful and reasonably angled climb (never greater than 7%) with some lovely views back over the Earn Valley, then a fast descent to meet the A823.

Here you turn right with another gradual ascent up Glen Devon, followed by a superb fast descent of Glen Eagles, to pass over the railway and the A9 and through the world famous golf courses. Turn right to Muirton, veer right at the next junction and go through the village.

Turn right at a T-junction, then left at the next one onto the A824 and follow it into Auchterarder and a post ride cake in one of the many cafés.

St Andrews

*A*s usual, whichever way the wind's blowing will probably determine the direction in which you tackle this circuit. It is described in an anti-clockwise, so the prevailing wind will probably be at your back on the latter part of the route.

Start from the car park, toilets and café off the B946 to Tayport, gained from the roundabout at the southern end of the Tay Road Bridge. The café is open from 8am to 5pm in the summer and closes at 4pm in the winter. If this location is too busy, then the first layby

(NO 435290) on the B946 east towards Tayport is close by, but unfortunately it doesn't have toilets.

Exit left from the bridge car park then left again onto the B946 to Newport on Sustrans Route 777. Pass under the bridge, continue through Newport, then climb through Wormit past the Tay Rail Bridge and take a right at the top of the hill, signposted to Gauldry. Where the Sustrans route goes off right, stay on the main road through Gauldry which is rejoined by the Sustrans route, then at a crossroads

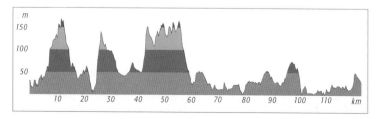

4km beyond Gauldry, turn right, sign-posted Newburgh and Scenic Route to Perth and Sustrans Route 777. This road takes you down to the shores of the Firth of Tay looking over the Carse of Gowrie with the Sidlaw Hills behind. On a clear day, two distinct mountains can be seen in the distance; Ben Vorlich and Stuc a' Chroin.

Arrive in Newburgh at a T-junction, turn right and head along High Street where there are a couple of cafés if refreshment is required. At the far end of High Street and almost opposite the war memorial, turn left (signposted Ninewells Farmhouse B&B) into Woodriffe Road – Sustrans Route 776.

This climbs fairly abruptly out of town to a fork in the road. Turn left and climb

up to join the B936 and a right turn to Auchtermuchty. The fork is just past a bench on your left where you might see some teddy bears sitting on a bench!

You'll come into Auchtermuchty past the Cycle Tavern on your left just before you reach the A91 – Cupar Road. Cross straight over, signposted for Falkland, heading towards West Lomond hill on the skyline to reach the A912. Turn left onto Sustrans Route 1 and skirt Falkland on this, turning left again onto the B936 to Freuchie. Falkland is worth a visit and has a palace, cafés and pubic toilets.

Go through Freuchie, over the A92 into Freuchie Mill Road which leads to the A914, crossed by a staggered right-left junction signposted Kennoway.

Another climb with some steep sections leads towards Milldeans. At the end of the long straight through woodland, turn left signposted to Kingskettle and Burnturk.

As you traverse Cults Hill there are some great views looking over the Eden Valley. Go straight on at the next crossroads, signposted to Largo. At the next junction ignore the cycle way signs and continue straight on to reach the A916.

If you wish to cut this route short you can follow the cycle way signs to Ceres and onwards to St Andrews and re-join the route there.

Turn right onto the A916 and follow this for about a kilometre before taking the next main turning left, signposted to Lundin Links and Largo. At the T-junction turn left and follow the A915 east through Lower Largo.

Continue east through Upper Largo towards Elie and Anstruther and enter the East Neuk of Fife, a beautiful coastal area interspersed with fishing villages stretching along the south coast of the region. It's worth taking the detours down through the villages to their pretty harbours, such as that at St Monans, although some of the ascents and descents are on the steep side. All are great places to stop for a café break and many have a public toilet near the harbour area.

In Anstruther turn right at the mini-roundabout and descend to the harbour where there are fine views out over the Firth of Forth past the Isle of May to the Bass Rock and East Lothian.

Where the main road bears left go straight on, signposted Cellardyke Harbour, passing through some narrow but scenic streets to reach the harbour. Beyond the harbour go left where the road forks and ascend past a caravan site. It's a bit of a rough track but doesn't last for long.

Anstruther harbour

On the South Fife coast

Follow the access road up to some traffic lights and turn right back onto the A917 for Crail. In Crail, the A917 swings sharply northwards then northwest to reach historic St Andrews. As you head through the town look out for signs for the A91 Tay Bridge.

At a large roundabout on the western edge of the town, take the right exit signposted for Hotel, Golf Courses and pass the Old Course Hotel and the legendary 18th hole of the Old Course. Just before the road rejoins the A91, turn right onto the cycle way and follow it west until it merges with the pavement near Guardbridge. Veer off right before the road bridge to cross the old single lane bridge alongside.

Turn right onto the A919 at the roundabout and the cycle way (Sustrans Route 1) continues on the pavement then crosses to its own tarmac route.

The cycle path can then be followed or the main road which is a lot less busier than the A91. Follow this road through Leuchars and on to St Michaels Inn. Turn right here onto the B945, which and follow it through Tayport and back to the Tay Road Bridge.

Lomond Hills Extension
You can make an extension to this route which climbs from the centre of Falkland village beside the Maspie Den to the col between East and West Lomond. It's a lovely climb that is never too steep, with a nice gradual descent on the other side. The only drawback is that the roads from Leslie to Freuchie are fast and busy.

As you come into Leslie, the road splits. Take the left fork up a short hill to a junction where you turn left onto the A911. Follow this to a large roundabout and turn left onto the B969. Go straight on over two more roundabouts and take a left onto the A92. A right onto the A914 at the next roundabout leads to the staggered junction just outside Freuchie where you can rejoin the route.
Distance 13km (8 miles); Height gain 250m (820ft); Max gradient 17%

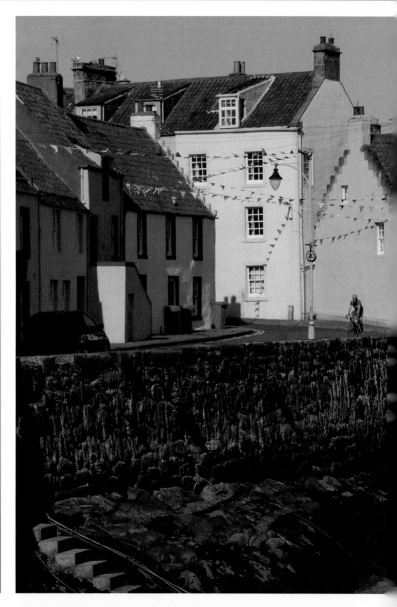

St Monans harbour

Around the Tay

A circuit round the firth, plus a hill or two

East over the Tay

Most of this route is on small rural roads with short sections, mainly on cycle routes, through Perth and Dundee. The route shares some of the roads on the south side of the Firth of Tay with the Kingdom of Fife [12].

A good starting place is the car park at the south end of the Tay Road Bridge, as for the previous route. Alternately you could start at Kinnoull Hill (see the end of the route).

Exit left from the bridge car park then left again onto the B946 to Newport on Sustrans Route 777. Pass under the bridge, continue through Newport, then climb through Wormit past the Tay Rail Bridge and take a right at the top

of the hill, signposted to Gauldry. Just outside Gauldry turn right and descend to Balmerino and the ruins of Balmerino Abbey and views over the Tay, then ascend back to the main road and turn right.

Continue to a crossroads and go right, signposted Newburgh and Scenic Route to Perth. Arrive in Newburgh at a T-junction and turn right onto the A913. Head through the town then Abernethy and Aberargie, this road can be busy during the morning or evening commute, to reach a roundabout.

Turn right onto the A912, then immediately left onto a minor road signed to Dron and continue to a T-junction. Go right and remain on this road to pass

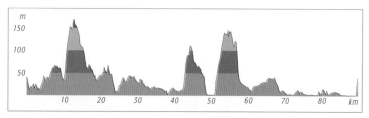

under the M90 to reach Bridge of Earn, where you go left onto the A912.

Head down Main Street, cross over the River Earn and turn right, sign-posted to Rhynd. The road goes back under the motorway and round the edge of Moncrieffe Hill before swinging north and climbing to the hamlet of Rhynd. Cross the high ground beyond, with views north to rocky Kinnoull Hill, before descending to pass over the motorway and rejoin the A912.

Turn right onto this for 600m, then take another right into Friarton Road, signposted Recycling Centre. Follow this down to the River Tay where it veers left through Perth's docklands.

Go straight on at a roundabout, under the railway bridge and on through two sets of traffic lights to the second bridge over the river. Just before you get there, cross to the riverside pavement and use this to access the bridge as you can't turn right at the road junction.

Cross over the bridge and back onto the road to gain the right-hand lane at the traffic lights (Ahead Only). You are going straight up the steep hill ahead (17%) so you need to select bottom

gear. This is Sustrans Route 77, the route to Dundee, which is well signed from this point.

As the road bears right the angle relents and emerges into rural Perthshire. A climb leads to the car park for Kinnoull Hill which offers an alternative start, but has the downside of an uphill finish.

Skirt the high ground, descend to a T-junction then go left and descend to Glencarse. This is steep and narrow, so take care. Go through Glencarse and over the A90 to St Madoes, then on through Errol following signs for Invergowrie.

On the outskirts of Invergowrie pass over the railway then watch out for Sustrans Route 77 signs pointing right down Station Road. Go past the station to just before joining Main Street where a signposted cycle way goes off right.

Follow this beside the A85 dodging the pedestrians, fishermen, other cyclists and penguins of the Dundee waterfront, to arrive at the Tay Bridge. And now for something completely different! A route with a lift which takes you up to the bridge and a very slightly uphill cycle back to Fife.

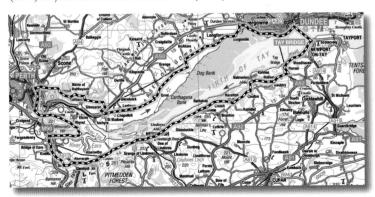

Perthshire

West to Kinloch Rannoch from the Schiehallion road

Perthshire and in particular Highland Perthshire is road biking heaven, combining quiet roads and stunning scenery. The landscape becomes more rugged as you travel north of the Highland Boundary Fault, the geological fault that separates Highland from Lowland Scotland. The hills get bigger (not necessarily the cycling ones) and are very popular with hillwalkers. Schiehallion is one of the better known peaks and dominates the area round Lochs Tummel and Rannoch.

Perthshire is a great area to start climbing in the hills as most are short and on the right side of 20%. The Etape Caledonia, the first and still one of the few closed road sportives in the UK, is staged in this area every spring and is hugely popular, attracting more

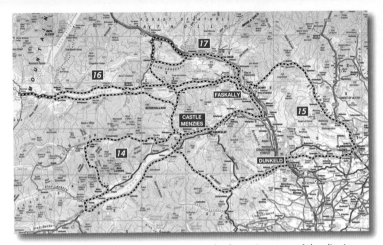

than 5,000 participants. Places sell out in hours! The week before the sportive, the Highland Perthshire Cycling Festival takes place and with events across the region on all things biking, it's well worth a look.

As a result of all this promotion, there are many more road cyclists out and about and it is unusual not to come across fellow cyclists any day of the

week. The main towns of the district, Aberfeldy, Dunkeld and Pitlochry, the latter two with very good bike shops, have all the usual amenities but can be very busy in the summer and at weekends.

The four routes in this chapter could be combined into much longer circuits should you want to cram a little bit more Perthshire magic into your day.

Schiehallion

Descending to Glen Lyon from the Bealach na Lairige

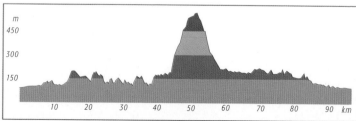

Ben Lawers dominates the northern side of Loch Tay and offers a high quality route with two very contrasting sections. The undulating southern part on Sustrans Route 7 is followed by a steep mountain pass over the Lawers range and down into Glen Lyon.

West of Aberfeldy is the hamlet of Weem and just beyond that is the entrance to Castle Menzies where there is a Forestry Commission car park. From the car park head west and take the minor road on your left signposted to Kenmore. Turn left and go through

the village. Where the main road turns left you take a right and follow the road along the southern shore of Loch Tay, past the Crannog centre. A very undulating experience, enhanced by great views of the hills on the north side of the loch – all the ingredients for a GWR.

Upon reaching Killin turn right onto the A827 and pass over the Falls of Dochart, which are more a series of rapids than waterfalls. Go through the village, there are plenty of opportunities for refreshment, and head back east along the north side of Loch Tay

After 7km you reach a minor road on

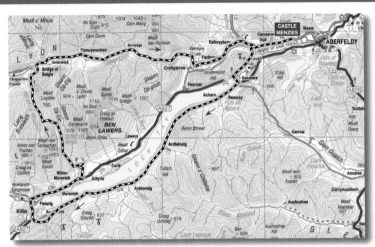

your left signposted to Bridge of Balgie. The gradient immediately increases (15%) and doesn't relent till you are out of the felled forestry and onto the open hillside above. After that it's a fairly gradual climb with a couple of steeper bits, past the dam and Lochan na Lairige, to the top.

A lovely flowing descent then follows down into Glen Lyon. An essential stop is the café at Bridge of Balgie at the bottom which serves food and cakes.

One of the great pleasures in life is sitting in the sun at the café having just hurtled down from Bealach na Lairige.

From here you head back, down scenic Glen Lyon. At the junction turn left through the picturesque village of Fortingall, said by some to be the birth place of one Pontius Pilate and also the site of the Fortingall yew, said by others to be the oldest living organism on the planet! This road takes you to the B846, where you turn right, back to Weem.

Falls of Dochart at Killin

Glen Quaich

A lovely mixture of highland and lowland Perthshire, this route involves some main roads but they are mostly quiet. The route starts in Dunkeld, another Perthshire village which can be very busy in at height of the summer. Having said that, it is a lovely place and the cathedral is well worth a visit. The car park at the north end of the town has toilets. There is a charge for toilets and parking.

From the car park head back through town and across Thomas Telford's

1809 bridge over the River Tay to reach the A9. Turn right then left onto the A822 signposted to Crieff and ascend gradually through Strathbraan to where the A826 to Aberfeldy is signposted on the right; a shorter alternative route via Glen Cochill, described at the end.

Continue on the A822 to just past the hamlet of Amulree and take the minor road on the right signposted to Glen Quaich. Be prepared for a wee toughie of a climb. The beautiful and isolated road up the glen is fairly benign at first.

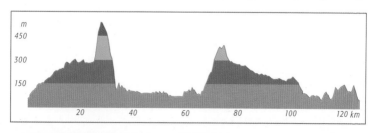

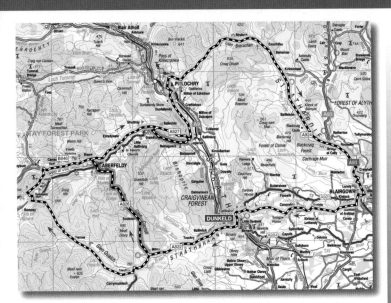

In the distance you'll see a strip of tarmac going up the right side of the glen and that's where you're heading. Once it kicks up it doesn't really relent for about 2.5km with 15% and a fair bit of 20% thrown in for good measure.

The top is a lovely place to take in the magnificent view of the Glen Lyon hills and get your breath back. The descent should be treated with caution as it is equally steep and narrow. At the bottom take a right then a left onto the A827 and go through Kenmore where there are a couple of cafés and a shop. Now on Sustrans Route 7, cross over the River Tay to a turning on the right, signposted Tummel Bridge and Kinloch Rannoch. Keep straight on along this road to reach the River Lyon and cross over to a junction with the B846. Turn right and follow this through Weem to

where it turns sharp right. Continue straight ahead on a minor road signposted to Strathtay; Sustrans Route 7.

Follow this to the A827 where there are two options. Turning left towards Ballinluig takes you off the Sustrans route and along the A827 for 4km to Logierait. The traffic can be fast but it's generally not too bad. Just before the Logierait Inn, turn north signposted Dunfallandy to rejoin Sustrans Route 7.

A quieter option is to remain on the Sustrans route. Turn right over the Tay on the A827, then left along the B898 to regain the A827 at Logierait via a disused rail bridge over the Tay. Follow the A827 left to the Dunfallandy turning, beyond the Logierait Inn.

Make sure you select your lowest gear before the Dunfallandy turning as there is a short, sharp and steep (20%) hill.

Continue over a couple of hills and under the A9 to a T-junction. Ignore the signs for the Sustrans cycle route and turn right over the River Tummel to reach the A924. Take a left turn here and head up and along Pitlochry's high street, where you'll find plenty of cafés.

In the centre of the town turn right on the A924 signposted to Blairgowrie and Braemar. This is a gradual and scenic climb out of town which takes you up and over the moor, before dropping down to Kirkmichael and straight on to Bridge of Cally. Here you turn right to join the A93 and a short gradual climb from the River Ardle

before descending into Blairgowrie where the A93 joins the A926.

Descend right and cross over the River Ericht to traffic lights, where the road forks. Take the left-hand fork and go up the short hill to a roundabout where you turn right signposted Perth and Dunkeld. At the top of the street turn left, back on to the A93. You'll pass a Co-op supermarket on your left and a bike shop on your right as you cycle along this road. Ignore the right turn onto the A923 signposted to Dunkeld and continue for about 500m where you turn right onto the B947 signposted to Lethendy.

The tough climb through Glen Quaich

Follow this to a turning on the right just after the bridge over the Lunnan Burn, signposted to Craigie. This leads to a T-junction and a left to Snaigow, then round the shores of Loch of Clunie to a crossroads. Go straight over and continue to a slight hill rising to a T-junction, where a sign indicates Dunkeld is only four and a half miles away.

Take a right to pass Loch of the Lowes where Ospreys regularly nest, then turn left onto the A923 to Dunkeld. A short flowing descent leads to the junction with the A984 where you turn left back to the start.

> **Glen Cochill Variation**
> *Turn right onto the A826 and make a gradual ascent up Glen Cochill, followed by a sweeping descent to Aberfeldy. Continue straight over onto the B846 signposted Weem and Kinloch Rannoch and cross the ornate 1733 'Wade' bridge over the Tay. Continue to the outskirts of Weem where the road makes a sharp left. Turn right here onto Sustrans Route 7, to rejoin the main route.*
> **Total distance 110km (68 miles); Height gain 1100m (3609ft); Max gradient 20%; Approx time 5hrs**

16 The Two Lochs
A circuit of Loch Tummel & Loch Rannoch

West to Loch Rannoch

N*ot too many hills on this route – honest! It's a bit lumpy at the beginning and the end, with a gradual climb in the middle. From Faskally head north on the B8019 (B8079) to a junction where the B8079 continues to Killiecrankie and turn left over the River Garry on the B8019. There are quite a few ups and downs alongside Loch Tummel but the views make up for it. It can be busy as far as the Queen's View at the start of Loch Tummel, but after that the road is usually pretty quiet.*

At Tummel Bridge turn right onto the B846 and follow this to Kinloch Rannoch where you'll find a café, shop and across the road, public toilets at the Dunalastair Hotel. The route continues round the north side of Loch

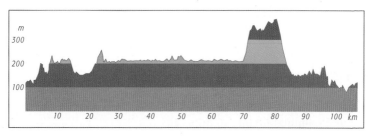

Rannoch. As you head west the view opens up and you should be able to make out the distant hills of the Black Mount and in particular Buachaille Etive Mòr at the entrance to Glen Coe.

The road round Loch Rannoch is one of the best family cycle routes in Scotland being relatively traffic free and with lots of places to stop and enjoy the view. A perfect place for a two day family adventure with a night out camping on the shores of the loch.

At the western end of Loch Rannoch, the road continues to Rannoch Station as detailed in the extension described at the end of this route. The return route turns left for Bridge of Gaur and South Loch Rannoch. Cross the bridge over the River Gaur and follow the minor road along the south shore to the east end of the loch, then take a small road which branches off right past houses and Bunrannoch House.

Bear right onto a minor road from Kinloch Rannoch and continue to

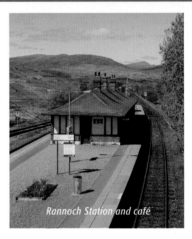

Rannoch Station and café

Dunalastair Water, beyond which the road starts to climb like a staircase under the shadow of Schiehallion. Higher up it levels out and there's even a wee bit of down before climbing again to the junction with the B846

Schiehallion from the east across Loch Tummel

Etape Caledonia at Kinloch Ranoch

and a left turn to Tummel Bridge. Fly down the hill, watch for grit on the descent, then just after a sharp left-hand bend, take another small road on the right signposted to Foss.

The Foss road is an excellent example of a GWR and the views are outstanding. A rollercoaster of a ride follows along the south side of Loch Tummel, then be prepared for a bit of up from the east end of the loch at Cluanie Dam. The next scenic section

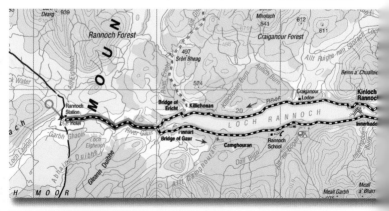

Loch Faskally in
autumn glory

undulates alongside the river gorge
and Loch Faskally until you arrive at the
A9. Here there are two options.

You can turn right onto the A9 which
you follow for about 500m to exit at
the next major junction on the left
(signposted B8019 Tummel Bridge and
Kinloch Rannoch), followed by a right
turn back to the parking at Faskally.

Alternatively, just before joining the
A9 take a small road on your left which
looks like it is a driveway into some-
body's house. This becomes a narrow
strip of tarmac running parallel to the
A9 and is followed round left onto a
road (Foss Road), which leads down
past Pitlochry Festival Theatre to a No
Through Road on the left, signposted
Port na Craig. Follow this down, you are

now on Sustrans Route 7, and cross the
footbridge over the River Tummel.

Follow the Sustrans cycle route signs
up to Pitlochry high street, turn left and
go through the town to pass under the
A9 back to the parking.

> ### Rannoch Station Extension
> *For those of you who want to stretch
> the legs a little more, take the road
> out and back to Rannoch Station at
> the west end of Loch Rannoch. As a
> reward (!) there is a great wee café
> at the station, normally open from
> March to October.*
> **Distance 17km (10.5 miles); Height
> gain 100m (328ft); Max gradient 10%**

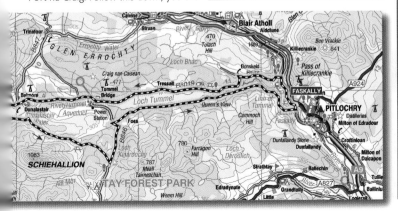

The finishing line of the Etape Caledonia in Pitlochry

A great introduction to the delights of Perthshire cycling, this is a delightful route, which if done anti-clockwise as described, has most of the climbing in the first half. From Faskally head north on the B8019 which transforms unannounced into the B8079 and continue through Killiecrankie and Blair Atholl to the House of Bruar shops and the Falls of Bruar. Before reaching the A9, turn right onto the B847, follow it to Calvine and turn left signposted to Tummel Bridge and Kinloch Rannoch. The extension to Dalnacardoch, described at the end of this route, finishes (or starts depending on direction) at the west end of Calvine, just before the A9.

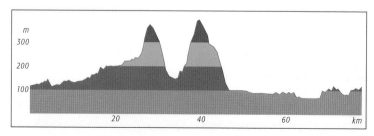

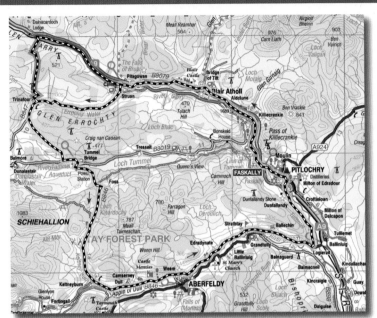

Pass over the River Garry and under the railway and climb gradually up Glen Errochty to a junction just before a bridge over the Errochty Water, where a minor road goes off right to Dalnacardoch, the extension described on the next page. Continue south on the B847 past Trinafour House, after which the climb is a bit steep (15%) but quickly relents. Keep climbing to a junction with a small road on the left signposted Tummel Bridge.

Ascend this and as you crest over the top the countryside opens out with views across the Tummel valley dominated by the pyramid of Schiehallion. The mountain's isolated position and regular shape was used by the Astronomer Royal, the Reverend Nevil Maskelyne to determine the Earth's mass back in 1774. Maskelyne and a team of surveyors and mathematicians spent four months working from a bothy near the summit. As part of the

Dalnacardoch Extension
*This little 'add-on' is best included in a clockwise version of Land of Atholl to give
a twisty ascent followed by a flowing descent, rather than the other way around
(although that does alter the dynamics of Land of Atholl too!). From Trinafour
turn left off the B847 onto a minor road signposted to Dalnacardoch. There is a
short level bit then the road climbs in a series of steps with some beautifully
re-engineered hairpin bends to where it relents and gradually climbs to the
summit for great views of Schiehallion and the surrounding hills. Another lovely
sweeping descent follows on the other side. Although there will be the usual
hordes of cyclist watching sheep, you may also come across red deer on this
section, especially in late autumn. At the bottom of the hill, rejoin the Sustrans
cycle route parallel to the A9 and follow it back to Calvine and Pitlochry.*
Distance 8km (5 miles); Height gain 200m (656ft); Max gradient 17%

process, matematician Charles Hutton
created a map linking points of equal
altitude around the mountain – the first
use of contours in Britain.

A sublime descent brings you to the
junction with the B846. Turn left to
Tummel Bridge and just before the
village, bear right over the River
Tummel and on past the hydro power
station. From here there's a pretty
steady climb up to Loch Kinardochy,
with one steepish bit at the first bend.
Another great descent follows (don't
get carried away) to Coshieville,

beyond which you join Sustrans Route
7 and continue east through Appin of
Dull to Weem. There are a couple of
cafés along this stretch of road, if you
think you deserve a break by now!

Beyond Weem the B846 makes a
sharp right. Continue straight ahead
here onto a minor road signposted to
Strathtay. Follow this to the A827
where there are two options. Turning
left towards Ballinluig takes you off the
Sustrans route and along the A827 for
4km to Logietait. The traffic can be fast
but it's generally not too bad. Just before

Climbing up from Trinafour in Glen Errochty

the Logierait Inn, turn north signposted Dunfallandy to rejoin Sustrans Route 7.

A quieter option is to remain on the Sustrans route. Turn right over the Tay on the A827, then left along the B898 to regain the A827 at Logierait via a disused rail bridge over the Tay. Follow the A827 left to the Dunfallandy turning, beyond the Logierait Inn.

Make sure you select your lowest gear before the Dunfallandy turning as there is a short, sharp and steep (20%) hill. Continue over a couple of hills and under the A9 to a T-junction. Ignore the signs for the Sustrans cycle route and turn right over the River Tummel to reach the A924. Take a left turn here and head up and along Pitlochry's high street where there are plenty of cafés if sustenance is required. Go through the town to pass under the A9 and back to the parking.

Blair Castle and Beinn a' Ghlo

Deeside &

Looking east over Loch Insh to the Glen Feshie hills

*N*orth and east of the hills of Perthshire lies the vast expanse of the Cairngorm Mountains, an area characterised by high arctic plateau, quite different to the more rugged peaks of the west coast. Much of this area is part of the Cairngorms National Park, the largest in the UK.

The first routes in this chapter start on the south side of the Cairngorms. The roads in this area don't tend to go through the mountains but round them, so any routes are generally long.

To 'do' the whole Cairngorm Brute circuit is a very big day and necessitates using the cycle route over Drumochter (not recommended on skinny tyres), unless you fancy dicing with death on the A9.

I would recommend using the train between Pitlochry and Aviemore for this route, but make sure you have a booking first. You can rid yourself of the organisational part of the cycle by signing up for the annual 3 Pistes Cycle Sportive <www.3pistescycle.co.uk> which has the added bonus(!) of finishing at the Cairngorm ski area car park. Most participants I talked to at the inaugural event in June 2014 said it was a brute of a route and I would agree with that.

Another lurking monster, (no, not the Loch Ness one), traverses the farmlands of Strathmore to Royal Deeside

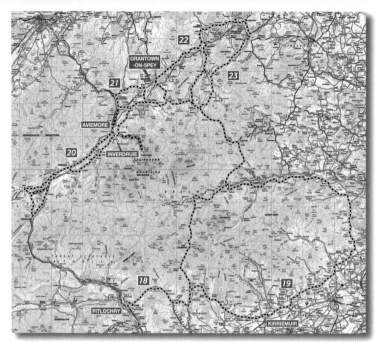

then climbs up through the wild open landscape of Glen Clunie, then down Glen Shee and back to rural Angus. However you can split the route into two days with a stopover in Ballater where there is a very good bunkhouse.

The four northern routes are generally not that hilly with the only 'big' climb being the road to the Cairngorm ski area. Inverdruie is a bit less busy than downtown Aviemore and is the starting point for the first two routes. Aviemore itself has full amenities including a very good bike shop, Mike's Bikes at the north end of the village.

The lower part of Strathspey is where a major part of the country's whisky production is concentrated. The last two routes in the chapter start near Grantown and venture into the eastern part of the northern Cairngorms on quiet but hillier minor roads.

Time for a pint?

18 Cairngorm Brute

A tough route with a brutish height gain

Above Cock Bridge and Corgaff Castle

Pitlochry or Aviemore can be used to start this route, combined with an outward or return journey by train, depending on the direction in which you want to tackle the Cairngorm Brute. Approaching from the north, the hills are marginally easier and not as sustained to begin with, but they are in the latter part. From the south, the section from Corgarff to the Lecht is the hardest.

The route is described here from south to north and there are plenty of spots for refreshment in villages along the way. There are also cafés at the Glenshee and Lecht Ski Centres and at Corgarff, Spittal of Glenshee and Bridge of Brown.

From Pitlochry Station, go north to the main street and turn right. At the next junction, just after a pedestrian crossing, take a left onto the A924 sign-posted to Moulin and Braemar and climb out of the town. It's not too steep, just a steady ascent up onto the moor, then down Glen Brerachan and

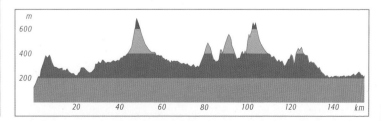

Chips, chips, gloroius chips

past Enochdhu to Kirkmichael. Just after Kirkmichael turn left onto the B950. At the next junction turn left onto the A93 and head north towards Glen Shee.

This road undulates along to the Spittal of Glenshee where, after a flattish section, the climb up to the head of Gleann Beag and the Glenshee Ski Centre begins. It's never steep but it just goes on and on at 12%. This part of the road used to be known as 'The Devil's Elbow' and if you look out to the right you'll see the old road. It is now known locally as 'The Slide' as some of the locals have used various objects to slide down the hill when it has been snowy or icy.

From the top it's a lovely long descent down Glen Clunie to Braemar. Continue through Deeside for another 14km

Speed at the Bridge of Brown

The climb to The Lecht – spot the cyclists

until just after Balmoral Castle, where a left turn onto the B976 leads over the flanks of Geallaig Hill (not too steep) to Gairnsheil Lodge. Another left turn, onto the A939, leads through the hills (getting steeper) and down to the River Don. At the T-junction, keep left on the A939 signposted to Tomintoul, and pass through Corgarff then over Cock Bridge and ascend past the snow gates to the Lecht Ski Centre (very much steeper). This is the well-known (or infamous) Cock Bridge to Tomintoul road! As you crest the initial twisty steep part (20%) and gaze at the tarmac rising ahead you may wonder 'How am I going to get up there?'. No-one said it was going to be easy!

Down towards Tomintoul the road undulates along and beyond this there is the dip of the River Avon to cross

and a steep climb out again at Bridge of Brown. About 7km after Bridge of Brown turn left onto a minor road which drops down towards Nethy Bridge. Just before Nethy the road splits, take the left fork, go over a crossroads and down into the village.

Take a left onto the B970, signposted to Coylumbridge and there are just a few short ups to go. At Coylumbridge take a right and go through Inverdruie and over the River Spey, to a roundabout at the southern end of Aviemore. Turn right here and the railway station is on the right.

If you want to cycle back to Pitlochry then it's another 60km and 430m of ascent on Sustrans Route 7 from Inverdruie. In the village turn left onto the B970 signposted to Feshiebridge and follow the Sustrans signposts.

The climb to Cairn o' Mount

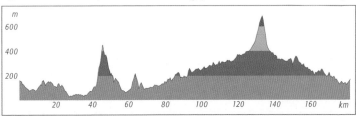

*A*t 190km this is a monster of a route, although the height gain and maximum gradient aren't as draining as the Cairngorm Brute. I have described it in an anti-clockwise direction since that's the only way I've done it, but there probably isn't much between them.

Kirriemuir's Camera Obscura is well signposted from the town and the car park has toilets as well. From the car park, exit back to West Hill Road. Turn right then immediately left into Muir

Road to reach a T-junction. Turn left and on to a crossroads, then a right and on past Kirriemuir Golf Club. Continue on this road for 9km, passing over the River South Esk to take a left turn signposted to Noranside, just before a white bungalow.

At the next crossroads take a right, signposted to Menmuir. Keep on this road and at the white war memorial, 400m after passing through the hamlet of Kirkton of Menmuir, take a left turn signposted to Edzell. Just after a sharp right bend, turn left to Edzell, crossing over the West Water to reach the town. Go left onto High Street and follow the B966 to Fettercairn, then the B974 signed to Cairn o' Mount and Banchory.

From the tea room at Clatterin' Brig the road rises steeply (16%) before flattening out a bit then rearing up again towards the summit of Cairn o' Mount. It's not that long an ascent and with fresh legs feels okay. There is a lovely view south over Strathmore to Montrose and the sea, followed by a great descent with a couple of short ups.

About 10km down this road at an old AA telephone box, take a left onto a minor road signposted to Aboyne. This leads to a junction with the B976 where you take a left heading past

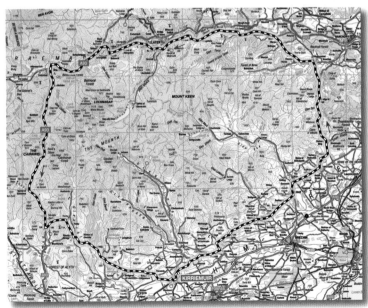

Aboyne and then Ballater on the south side of the River Dee. There are few hills in this section but you are gradually climbing all the way to the Glenshee Ski Centre beyond Braemar. As some form of compensation you'll get great views of the Deeside hills, particularly Lochnagar. There are a number of good cafés in Ballater and an excellent chip shop in Braemar. These villages also have public toilets.

Join the A93 just after passing the entrance to Balmoral. It's a pretty quiet road, although there can be a bit of tourist traffic during the summer months. Once past Braemar the roads are usually very quiet, but the angle starts to steepen as you climb up Glen Clunie to the summit of the Cairnwell Pass, the highest main road in the UK. At the top is the Glenshee Ski Centre and another café, if you manage to get

Looking up Gleann Beag towards the Cairnwell Pass and the Glenshee Ski Centre

there before it closes for the day!

Then it's down 'The Slide' as it's known locally and Gleann Beag, past the Spittal of Glenshee Hotel and on for another 8km to a left turn onto the B951 to Glenisla and Kirriemuir. After a climb out of Glen Shee, this road gradually descends, although there are quite a few up bits where tired little legs are sure to start protesting. Once you can see the Sidlaw Hills in the distance you are nearly there – phew! A case of 'mind over matter'.

Take a left at the T-junction on the edge of Kirriemuir onto the B955 sign-posted Cortachy and Town Centre, then left at the next, signposted Cortachy. The fourth turning on the right leads into Angle Road which is followed to a crossroads. Go straight over into West Hill Road and follow the signs for the Camera Obscura.

Approaching Loch Insh

*I*nverdruie is the starting point for this lovely scenic route round the 'top end' of Strath Spey. From the car park opposite the Rothiemurchus Visitor Centre head north towards Aviemore on the B970. The visitor centre has an excellent café, one of my favourites, and toilets.

At the roundabout turn left onto the the B9152 and go through Kincraig to meet the A86 at Kingussie and join Sustrans Route 7. This goes off-road on the left, about 200m beyond the end of the village, and you can either follow that or remain on the A86 to Newtonmore. The Sustrans route has two right angles at the start which can be avoided by joining it about 300m further on.

In Newtonmore you'll pass the superb Highland Folk Museum on your left. It's one of the finest museums of its type and it's free. At the far end of the village keep left on the B9150, head south towards the A9 and pass over the River Spey. Just before this road joins the A9 turn right onto the No Through Road, signposted to the Ralia Café.

Continue straight on at the café

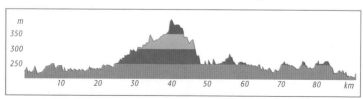

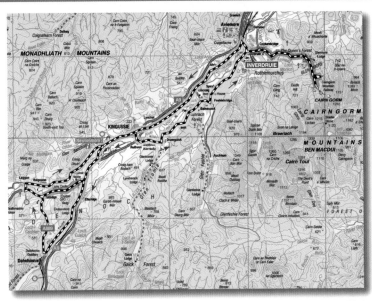

Taking a breather near Dalwhinnie

The Cairn Gorm ski road and Coire an Lochain

(another personal favourite) following the access road from the A9. The cycle route splits off to the right and leads to a minor road signposted Glentruim and Laggan, where there are two options. If you wish to shorten the route by about 8km, turn right here and cycle past the Invernahavon Caravan Site to Catlodge on the A889, via what is usually a very quiet road. This road goes past the old centre of Scotland, marked with a cross on a drystane dyke on the north side of the road, about 100m before the Macpherson monument and viewpoint.

Otherwise, continue past the Glentruim turning onto a road signposted to Crubenmore. Turn right, pass over the railway and keep straight ahead on the old A9 to Dalwhinnie. A gradual climb across the moor leads to a junction just before the village. Turn right onto the A889 to Laggan and

head up the short steepish hill to fine views over the Monadh Liath mountains, before plunging down on a roller coaster of a road to Catlodge.

Beyond Catlodge the road flattens out and there is a convenient café on your right, the Pottery Bunkhouse. At the junction with the A86 take a right to Laggan, cross back over the River Spey and continue through Newtonmore to Kingussie. Just as you come into Kingussie take a right onto the B970 signposted Ruthven and Sustrans Route 7. Cross over the railway and the River Spey and under the A9, then past the domineering ruins of Ruthven Barracks.

There is another shortish hill just before the car park for the walks and hides of the RSPB Insh Marshes National Nature Reserve. The marshes are one of the most important wetland

areas in Europe and well worth a visit.

Cross the River Tromie, then northwards through Insh and over the River Feshie at Feshiebridge. Continue northwards on the B970 back to Inverdruie passing the Inshriach Nursery. This gives you another chance to fuel-up at the coffee shop which is famous for its cakes. At the T-junction in Inverdruie, turn left back to the car park.

Cairn Gorm Extension

If you have a masochistic bent you can always add on a 'wee' trip up to the Cairngorm mountain railway and ski car park – the Alpe D'Huez of Scotland! From the car park in Inverdruie turn right and head along to Coylumbridge. From here it's a gradual climb then a fairly flat section along the shores of Loch Morlich, before you reach the snow gates at Glenmore where the real climbing begins. There is a steep section just before the road comes out of the trees, at what is known locally as the Sugar Bowl. After that the road turns east and flattens out (much to your relief). Another couple of steep bits and a final struggle (usually into the wind) and you are in the car park. Watch out on the way down as there tends to be quite a bit of grit at the first few bends.

There is a formal event, usually held in September, organised by the Cairngorm Cycle Club. One of the events that weekend is a time trial to the car park.

Distance 14km (8 miles), to the car park; Height gain 400m (130ft); Max gradient 15%

The Four Bridges

An historic tour of Speyside's bridges

South to the Cairngorms from the back road to Coylumbridge

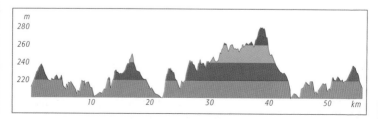

*N*ot surprisingly perhaps, four Speyside villages named after bridges feature in this undulating route along minor roads north-east from Aviemore. Anyone wanting a shorter day of about 15km with a little bit of up, can turn left into Boat of Garten and take the steam train back to Aviemore.

The car park in Inverdruie is opposite the Rothiemurchus Visitor Centre which has an excellent café, one of my favourites, and toilets. Turn right and head east on the B970 towards

Coylumbridge (the first bridge). Cross the bridge over the River Druie then turn left, still following the B970, sign-posted Boat of Garten.

Continue up the Spey valley to the left turn to Boat of Garten, then on for another 1km and take a right turn to Loch Garten. This leads through a large area of forestry including remnants of the Caledonian pine forest of Abernethy. It's a lovely section round Loch Garten and through the tall Scots Pines, but watch out for red squirrels! Go straight on at any junctions until you

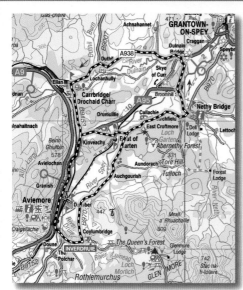

and over the railway leads to the A95 and a right turn towards Grantown-on-Spey. This can be a busy road but there is plenty of space for traffic to pass.

After 1km turn left, sign-posted Auchendean Lodge, onto a small road running parallel with the A95, then left again at the next junction and on to reach Dulnain Bridge (the third bridge). Cross the River Dulnain via Joseph Mitchell's 1830 stone bridge and turn left onto the A938 to reach Carrbridge (the fourth bridge). Turn left, sign-posted Aviemore, and cross the modern bridge over the River Dulnain, which gives fine views of John Niccelstone's single arch 1717 packhorse bridge.

As you pass through the village there is a good café (The Old Bakery) on the left-hand side and a short distance further on, there is a large car park with toilets. From Carrbridge it's back towards Aviemore along the B9153, to a junction with the A95, where you have a choice. You can take the direct variation south along the A95 to Aviemore, but it can be busy so take care.

If you wish to avoid this, turn left for a short distance on the A95 (there is also a parallel cycle path) before taking a right to Boat of Garten. After passing through 'the Boat' and over the Spey on a modern road bridge you reach the B970. Turn right and retrace your outward route to Coylumbridge and Inverdruie.

come to a T-junction in Nethy Bridge (the second bridge).

Turn right back onto the B970 and head through the village. Just before the hump-back bridge over the River Nethy, there is a shop on the corner on the right with picnic tables on the grass above the river. About 50m further down this road on the right is Nethybridge Community Centre which has signposted toilets to its right.

Cross Thomas Telford's fine 1810 bridge over the River Nethy and take an immediate left heading north to cross the River Spey by John Mackenzie's 15 span Broomhill Bridge. Although partly rebuilt in 1987, this trestle timber bridge dates from 1894 and is the oldest wooden road bridge still in service in Scotland.

A short climb past Broomhill Station

Autumn on the return route to Grantown-on-Spey

ast of Grantown-on-Spey, the Hills of Cromdale separate Strath Spey from Strath Avon and Glen Livet. This route circum-navigates the hills in an anti-clockwise direction starting with a climb over the southern end of the range to gain Strath Avon. **Around Ben Rinnes [23]** starts from the same point and is a longer circuit.

From the parking area turn right onto the A95, follow it to a roundabout and turn right towards Tomintoul. Cross over the River Spey and after about 1km take a right onto the A939, sign-posted to Tomintoul. Climb gradually to the high point of the route from where it's steeply downhill into the gash of Bridge of Brown. Beyond this a short brutish hill (20%) announces your arrival into Moray 'malt whisky country' and the Glenlivet Estate, followed by a steady descent to the Bridge of Avon (pronounced ann). Cross over the River Avon and turn left onto the B9136 to Bridgend of Glenlivet.

Follow Strath Avon with fine views west to the Hills of Cromdale, down through the hamlet of Glenlivet and over the River Livet to the junction with

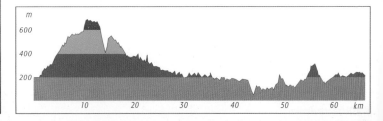

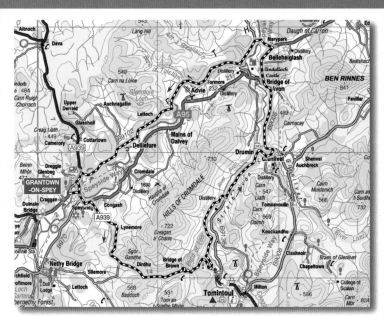

the B9008. Turn left, signposted to Craigellachie, and continue down Strath Avon to a junction with the A95 then go right on that road for about 3.5km to Marypark. Turn left here onto the B9138, signposted Knockando.

A short descent leads to a bridge over the River Spey, then a sharp climb to a T-junction where you turn left onto the

B9102. This very quiet and scenic road undulates alongside the River Spey all the way back to Grantown.

When you reach the town turn left and head along High Street to the second set of traffic lights where you turn left, signposted to Tomintoul. At the roundabout turn right onto the A95 and back to the starting point.

River Spey near Hill of Dalnapot

*Glen Livet and its
famous distillery*

*I*f you fancy something more challenging then you can extend the **Tour of the Cromdales [22]** by utilising further quiet and scenic roads to the east. It's only 35km longer but it's nearly double the amount of climbing! You can take your mind off matters by counting the number of distilleries you pass; there's quite a few.

From the parking area turn right onto the A95, follow it to a roundabout and turn right towards Tomintoul. Cross over the River Spey and after about 1km take a right onto the A939, sign-posted to Tomintoul. Climb gradually to the high point of the route from where it's steeply downhill into the gash of

Bridge of Brown.

Beyond this a short brutish hill (20%) announces your arrival into Moray 'malt whisky country' and the Glenlivet Estate, followed by a steady descent to cross the Bridge of Avon (pronounced ann) and on to Tomintoul.

The A939 passes through the village and where it turns off right, go straight ahead, now following the B9008 to Dufftown. Pass through Tomnavoulin in Glen Livet to Auchbreck and turn right onto the B9009; turning left joins the **Tour of the Cromdales [22]**. Climb up and over to Dufftown past Ben Rinnes and the Allt-a-Bhainne Distillery.

In Dufftown there are plenty of

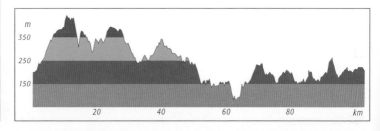

whisky shops but more importantly there is a café or two. Go straight on down the main street past the clock tower and onto the B9014, signposted to Keith. Continue on past a left turn to the Glenfiddich Distillery on the B975. It's one of the most popular distilleries to visit as the basic tour is free.

Remain on the B9014, crossing the River Fiddich to pass under a railway bridge and a short distance further on, turn left signposted to Maggieknockater (good name!). This great wee bit of road passes through some lovely beech forest, a total contrast to the wild moorland you have been through.

On reaching the A95, turn left and head for Craigellachie. There is a small shop here (the post office) and a small shop in Archiestown further on, but not much else between here and Grantown. There are public toilets on the left, just before you reach the A941.

Turn right onto the A941 and cross the River Spey with views of Thomas Telford's famous 1815 cast iron bridge, then turn off left onto the B9102, signposted Knockando. The route starts climbing past the Macallan Distillery onwards to Archiestown then undulates above the River Spey until it descends to join the **Tour of the Cromdales** [22] and follows the river back to Grantown.

On reaching the town, turn left and along High Street to the second set of traffic lights. Turn left here, signposted Tomintoul. At the roundabout turn right onto the A95 and back to the start.

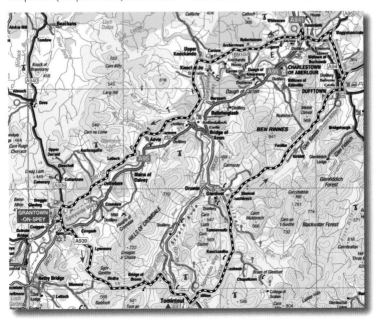

Inverness & Moray Coast

A forgotten corner of Nairnshire beside the River Findhorn

*I*nverness, the capital of the Highlands, is a pretty busy place throughout the year, but most of this revolves around the compact city centre. Just a stone's throw away you can find some very quiet roads through scenic countryside.

South of the city and east of Loch Ness lies a maze of deserted minor roads which feel wild and isolated. Even in the height of summer the traffic is fairly minimal and a complete contrast to the A82 on the west bank of the loch.

This road is very busy all through the year, so while the east side of Loch Ness offers pleasant cycling, the west side along the A82 cannot be recom-

mended. The west side does have the Great Glen Cycle Way, but it's designed for bikes with fatter tyres. If you really want to ride round the loch using the A82, then the best solution is to wait for the Etape Loch Ness. This closed road sportive first took place in May 2014 and may become an annual event.

Immediately east of Inverness lies the Moray Coast. It is very sheltered from the prevailing south-westerly weather and one of the driest areas in Scotland. If there is any chance of the sun shining, then the Moray Coast is the place to be.

North of Inverness on the other side of the Kessock Bridge is the Black Isle. In fact it is not an island at all, but a

fertile peninsula sandwiched between the Beauly and Moray Firths and the Cromarty Firth.

There are a number of possible explanations for the name. One is that it looks black when viewed from the surrounding snow covered higher ground in winter; another is its association with witchcraft in medieval times. Whatever its origins, the Black Isle offers great cycling beside and overlooking the sea.

24 Looking Over Loch Ness

Nessie watching away from the crowds

The view south-west down Loch Ness

Wild and generally deserted roads are a feature of this route which explores the countryside south of Inverness, between the Monath Liath mountains and the east bank of Loch Ness. The network of minor roads in this area means there are lots of variations possible, including the longer Garbole Road extension described at the end.

The route is best tackled in an anti-clockwise direction, partly to do with the prevailing south-west wind, but mainly so that you can get maximum benefit on the descents. Going the other way, the descents require a bit more caution.

Start from a small parking area at Littlemill, accessed from the A9 some 10km south of Inverness and just south of Daviot. From the A9, follow the B851 signposted to Fort Augustus for about 1.5km. Go past a Forestry Commission sign for Littlemill and 500m further on there is limited parking (marked on the OS 1:25k map), at a gated track into forestry.

Once on your bike, head south-west

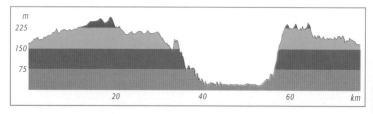

through Inverarnie then Farr towards Errogie and Fort Augustus. This area feels wild and remote with the mass of the Monadh Liath mountains dominating the views to the south, as you gradually ascend Strathnairn past the crags of Brin Rocks. At a T-junction with the B862, turn left and go through Errogie, from where a gradual descent is made past Loch Mhòr to a right turn onto the B852, signposted to the Falls of Foyers and Foyers.

This single track road initially winds its way through broadleaf woodland before descending beside the

River Foyers to the village of Foyers which lies on a ridge above Loch Ness. There is a shop, café and toilets at the top of the hill, before the descent to the village.

The trees open up as you descend to the lochside and eventually you get views of the surrounding countryside and the loch and the opportunity to stop and do a bit of Nessie spotting! Follow the lochside road which is nice and flat and pass through the village of Dores, beyond which the road leaves the shore and ascends, giving some spectacular views south-west

River Findhorn near Tomatin

Monarch of the Glen

down the Great Glen Fault, highlighting the vast extent of Loch Ness.

About 1.8km after Dores and about 500m beyond Aldourie Primary School, turn right onto a small unsignposted road leading past Darris. This is fairly flat at the start, but then it rears up just where it veers right, and for the next 5km climbs away from the loch at a fairly constant angle. In the spring, with no foliage on the trees, there are some lovely views over Loch Ness.

At the crossroads go straight over and head past Loch Ashie. Enjoy the tarmac twists and turns and the boulder-strewn landscape as the road weaves its way round the shores of Loch Duntelchaig and Loch Chlachain.

Go straight on at any road junctions to meet the B861 at Balnafoich. Turn right and head over the River Nairn to Inverarnie. Turn left here, onto the B851 and back to the car park.

Garbole Road Extension

This extension follows a very quiet and scenic road over to Strathdearn and the River Findhorn. Instead of turning left at Inverarnie, turn right and follow the B851 through Farr to a left turn onto a minor road signposted to Garbole. Follow this past Loch Farr. Just after you come out of the wood the road starts climbing fairly gradually with the odd steep (17%) bit. As you crest over the moor you'll become aware of the 'clutter' from our need for electricity. On the other side the descent requires a bit of caution and a couple of gates to open.

After arriving at the River Findhorn turn left and head down the glen to meet the old A9 at Findhorn Bridge and turn left through Tomatin. There is a small shop and café here if you are in need of sustenance. Follow the road to where it turns into Sustrans Route 7 north to Inverness, initially on the west side of the A9, then crossing to the east, to join the B9154. Continue round past Loch Moy and as the road comes back towards the main A9 at Daviot it descends to a junction, where the cycle route goes right, signposted to Culloden, Inverness and Dalroy.

Continue straight on for the A9 to arrive at a war memorial on the left and a No Through Road, signposted Daviot Farms Ltd. Follow this to a tunnel under the A9 and then up onto the B851. Turn right and it's a short distance back to the car park. This extension also makes a pleasant short circuit on its own, starting from Littlemill.

**Total distance 107km (64.5 miles); Height gain 750m (2461ft);
Max gradient 17%; Approx time 4hr 30min**

*Crossing the River Findhorn
at Dulsie Bridge*

O n the coast of the Moray Firth just to the east of Inverness, lies the town of Nairn. This circuit follows the course of the River Findhorn south to the edge of the northern Monadh Liath mountains, before returning to the coast. A large part of the route is through woodland, so it is fairly well protected if there is a strong wind blowing.

Approaching Nairn on the A96 from Inverness, the road turns sharp right at a roundabout and crosses the River Nairn. Turn left just after the bridge, signposted to parking at The Maggot and East Beach, and follow the road down to The Maggot car park opposite the harbour. There are public toilets

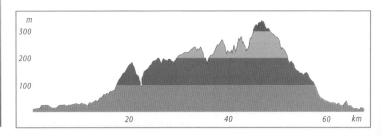

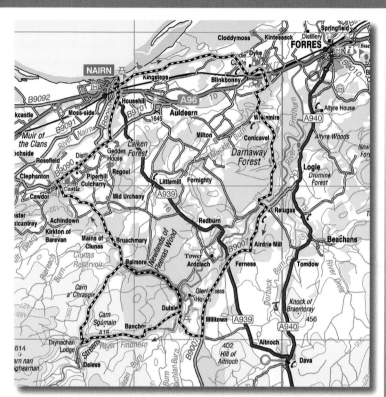

on the other side of the pedestrian bridge leading to the harbour and a nice wee café if you wish a post-ride refreshment.

Once on your bike, head back to the A96, turn left then left again at the traffic lights onto Lochloy Road (Sustrans Route 1), and follow this out of town past Nairn Dunbar Golf Club. After 9km you take a right, signposted to Brodie Castle, which you will glimpse through the trees on the left as you cycle past.

Just before you reach a level-crossing and the A96 take a left, signposted Dyke and Kintessack, go past the entrance to Brodie Castle and on to a four-way junction at a second castle entrance. Turn right here (Sustrans Route 1 continues ahead) signposted Forres and Nairn and cross the bridge over the railway to reach the A96.

Cross this busy road taking the minor road on the other side, signposted to Conicavel. At a T-junction turn right signposted Darnaway to gain open farmland. Take the next left signposted Conicavel, climb gradually up through beech trees to Conicavel and into the conifers of Darnaway Forest, before descending to a T-junction by the River Findhorn. Turn left, cross the Daltullich Bridge over the river and ascend to a junction with the B9007.

Turn right and continue to Ferness to meet the A939. Cross straight over, signposted Carrbridge, and carry on to a crossroads where you take a right to Dulsie Bridge and descend back to the River Findhorn. A short, sharp climb up and out of the river gorge brings you to a junction and a choice of routes to Balmore.

Straight ahead is less distance and climbing and offers a bit more shelter if it is windy. Turning left, signposted to Drynachan and Drynachan-Daless, takes in a lovely forgotten part of Nairnshire and the delights of a GWR. At Drynachan Lodge the route takes a sharp right, climbs out of the valley of the River Findhorn and over the moor to Balmore.

Beyond Balmore, keep straight on at any junctions, following the signs for

Approaching Cawdor village

Drynachan Lodge above the River Findhorn

Cawdor. A gentle descent leads past Cawdor Castle, perhaps best known for its literary connection to William Shakespeare's tragedy MacBeth, to meet the B9090 east of Cawdor village. There's a nice wee café on the left just before the junction if you are in need of refreshment.

Turn right onto the B9090 heading for Nairn and follow the road for 4km to a junction where the B9090 takes a left. Go straight on (now on the B9101 signposted Auldearn) and after another kilometre you come to a minor road on your left, signposted Sustrans Route 1. Follow this to a junction with the A939, turn left and on into Nairn to a T-junction with traffic lights. Turn left, pass under the railway bridge and straight on through a second set of traffic lights at Lochloy Road. The next right leads back to The Maggot car park.

Brodie Castle

The Black Isle
via the Moray, Beauly & Cromarty firths

Beside the Beauly Firth

Almost completely surrounded by the sea, the Black Isle offers fine cycling with open views and an ever changing seascape from dolphins to cruise liners and oil rigs!

Just after crossing the Kessock Bridge going north on the A9 from Inverness, follow the first slip road signposted Dolphin & Seal Visitor Centre and Tourist Information, to a car park with toilets.

Once on your bike, head out towards the A9 and pick up a cycle way on the left which runs alongside the A9. Turn left, signposted to Charleston, and descend to the road beyond a round-about. Continue down the road towards the sea to a turning on the right with signposts to Charleston and a Sustrans cycle route to Muir of Ord.

This gains a lovely stretch of road along the shores of the Beauly Firth and it's a shame it's not longer. Too soon it turns away from the sea and starts to go uphill. Take the first left and follow this till you come to a junction

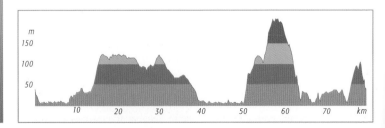

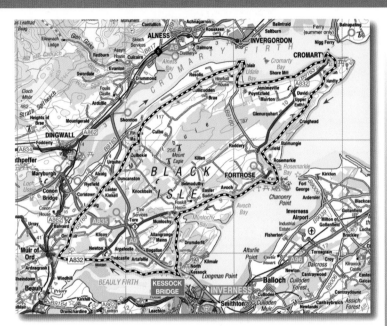

with the A832, where you turn left towards Muir of Ord; now on Sustrans Route 1.

Before reaching Muir of Ord you will arrive at a staggered crossroads where you take a right onto the B9169 to Culbokie. Turn right then left at the junction with the A835 and the same at the A9 beyond to reach Culbokie.

Pass through the village and as the road gradually gains height the views open up over the Cromarty Firth to the bulk of Ben Wyvis beyond. The B9169 becomes the B9163 and turns south at Balblair. Here a short variation is possible by turning left to Newhall Point and descending to the shore. The sea scenery can change a lot here, as the firth is often busy both with big

cruise ships using the pier over the water in Invergordon, and oil rigs berthed up for maintenance. Continue on this minor road to where it rejoins the B9163 and turn left.

In the distance, about 8km away on the right-hand headland at the mouth of the firth, is the village of Cromarty – your next destination. Go along the sea-front at Cromarty and turn up right, just beyond The Royal Hotel. Go past a café and toilets on the right, then through the village with a bakery and shop to reach a T-junction. There are now two options.

Turn left and head down the High Street and past a café to the sea where the road bears right, along the sea front. The road then swings left and

there is a sign indicating that the continuation (Miller Road) is a No Through Road. Don't worry about that – it's just a twisty road unsuitable for

coaches. Continue ahead and the road bears right again, then starts to climb to a T-junction where you take a right, then straight on, onto a rusty coloured, gravel farm access road. It's not that rough and I've never had a puncture on it although it wouldn't be very nice immediately after or during rain. Follow this for about 1.2km to a T-junction with a minor road (to Navity and Eathie) coming up from the A832 and turn left.

Alternatively, if you don't fancy the farm road, turn right at the T-junction in Cromarty, signposted Rosemarkie and follow the A832 to just beyond the farm at Newton of Cromarty. Turn left here onto the minor road signposted Navity and Eathie.

Whichever your approach, you climb up and over the spine of the Black Isle on this minor road and head south-

West along the Beauly Firth towards the mountains of Strathconnon

A832 but it is narrow so take care. Once at the A832 turn left to Rosemarkie; the Sustrans route goes right.

In the centre of Rosemarkie, take a left after The Plough Inn and descend to the sea, then go right and round Rosemarkie Bay, before bearing right and up to a T-junction. Turn left here and take the road through the golf course to the lighthouse at Chanonry Point for some dolphins, or turn right onto Ness Road and back to the A832.

Head left on the A832 through Fortrose and Avoch until you come to a junction with the B961, signposted to Munlochy. Briefly rejoin Sustrans Route 1 and head downhill then out of Munlochy, past where the Sustrans route heads off right, to where the road bears sharply right. Shortly after this, turn left at a war memorial onto a minor road signposted Drumsmittal.

A short gradual climb is followed by a descent towards the shores of the Cromarty Firth. As you come down the hill towards the A9 change down your gears; you turn right here signposted to North Kessock and Charleston and climb a short hill.

Follow the road round and under the A9 to a roundabout and take the first exit. Immediately on your right is the cycle way which will take you back to the car park from whence you started.

west. The road provides a spectacular viewing balcony over the Moray Firth with Ben Rinnes away to your left and the Cairngorms in the distance. Down below you can see Chanonry Point, a great place to go dolphin watching. The road has a very long descent to the

Cruise ship at Invergordon on the Cromarty Firth

West & North-west Coast

Below Bealach na Bà

Scotland's west & north-west coast is dramatic. A backdrop of mountains rising straight out of island-studded seas, along with some of the best beaches in the world. A wild place on the edge of Europe where the weather can be as dramatic as the scenery.

I have cherry-picked four circuits, each with its own unique character and challenge, spread along the coast from Moidart in the south to Assynt in the north. Included in these diverse routes are Màm Ràtagan near Glen Shiel and the Bealach na Bà near Applecross; two of the most iconic road climbs in the UK.

Outside of high summer, these roads range from very quiet to dead quiet and they can feel very remote, so the watchword up here is 'be prepared'. On many sections of these routes there will be no phone signal and it could be a while before help arrives in the shape of a passing car.

These routes will give you a flavour of the area and be etched into your memory long after the ride. You'll want to return time after time and check out all the corners of this fantastic part of Scotland. And there is more here than we can be covered in this guidebook; from a multi-day tour of the Outer Hebrides to the big landscapes of the north coast.

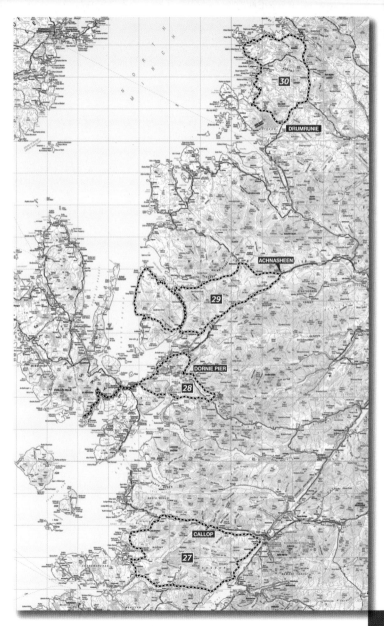

Ben Nevis from Loch Linnhe

West of Fort William lie the wild lands and sea lochs of Moidart and Ardgour. This stunningly scenic route has a few climbs, but fortunately none are very long, although a couple are a bit 'sharp'.

From Fort William, follow the A830 west towards Mallaig. Continue past Kinlocheil to the end of Loch Eil then, 3.5km past the turn-off on the left for the A861 to Strontian (the return), pass beneath a railway bridge. About 350m further on, at the apex of a wide bend, turn off left onto a track. Follow this for 200m, crossing a bridge over the Callop River, to reach a car park on the right.

Return to the A830 and follow the road west for 2.5km to Glenfinnan at the head of Loch Shiel passing the monument to commemorate the Jacobite clansmen and the place where Bonnie Prince Charlie raised his standard at the start of the ill-fated 1745 Jacobite Rising. There is a National Trust for Scotland Visitor Centre here with facilities. On the right you will also pass the iconic 21 arch curved viaduct which carries the West Highland Railway. Climb uphill then descend to pass along the north side of Loch Eilt to Lochailort, where you turn left onto the A861 signposted Glenuig and Strontian.

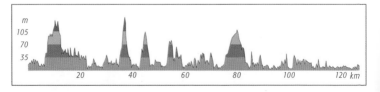

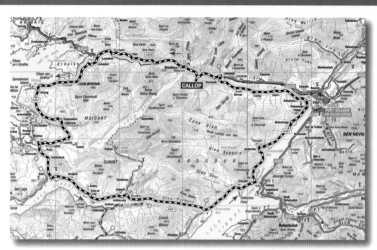

The road now becomes very much quieter and consists of a mix of dual and single track. Take care especially descending the single track as you never know what's round the corner – chances are it will be big and in the middle of the road!

As you come round Loch Ailort the mountain Rois-Bheinn towers above the road. At the headland before the road turns inland at Glenuig, there are great views out west to the sharp-profiled islands of Eigg and Rum, and north to the rocky coastline of Arisaig.

At Glenuig there is café at the Glenuig Inn over on the right, just before the

Glenuig & Loch Ailort

start of the climb up Glen Uig to Bealach Carach. From the top of the pass, the road descends to the shore of Loch Moidart and past information boards and a roadside cairn to the Seven Men of Moidart. This was a row of seven beech trees (no longer all there) planted to commemorate the seven men, four Irish, two Scots and one English, who accompanied Bonnie Prince Charlie prior to him raising the standard at Glenfinnan.

Cross the girder bridge over the river at Kinlochmoidart and climb through a section of broadleaf and conifer woodland to reach the open hillside and Captain Robertson's cairn, or rather the three of them; memorials to an eminent local. Descend the other side to Loch Shiel and cross the imposing three arched Shiel Bridge to Acharacle where there is a community run café and toilets.

Another climb leads over to Salen and Loch Sunart where the road weaves and bobs east along the side of the loch to Strontian where there are also toilets and a café.

A long gradual climb (another one!) leads up through an increasingly mountainous Glen Tarbert. If the prevailing wind is blowing, it might feel as if you have a little assistance. A great descent follows to the shores of Loch Linnhe with superb views straight across to the hills of Glen Coe. There is a shop in Clovullin if you have need of sustenance and a toilet a little further on at the Corran ferry.

The remaining section of single track road, north along Loch Linnhe and west along Loch Eil, has little traffic and offers superb views to the surrounding mountains and the vast bulk of Ben Nevis above Fort William.

Turn left along the A830 to regain the start, taking care at the narrowing under the railway bridge.

Loch Moidart

Zooming down Glen Tarbert to Loch Linnhe

The village of Duirinish

7his delightful route is mostly on minor roads and includes a couple of hills, a small ferry across the strait of Kyle Rhea to Skye and spectacular views. Some 18km is on the A87 which can be busy especially in the height of summer, but I've never found the traffic a problem.

The best place to start is near the village of Dornie on the A87. As you head west along the shore of Loch Duich and Loch Alsh towards Kyle of Lochalsh, you pass Eilean Donan Castle after which the road crosses a bridge over the foot of Loch Long. Dornie Pier

car park is on the left just after the bridge and has public toilets and a nice view of the castle.

From the car park, head east on the A87, back over the bridge and past the castle towards Shiel Bridge, getting your legs nicely warmed up for what is to come! At Shiel Bridge you take a minor road to the right, signposted to Glenelg and the Glenelg-Kylerhea car ferry.

The route now heads up and over the famous Màm Ràtagan pass to Glenelg; another cracking example of a GWR. It's a steady climb with a steeper sustained section in the upper half (15%), with

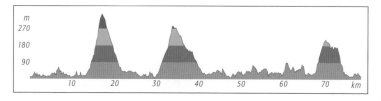

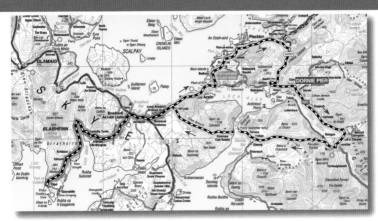

outstanding views of the Five Sisters of Kintail (the ridge of mountains to the east) and down to Loch Duich. Follow the road down towards Glenelg, turning right where it forks (signposted Galltair and Ferry). If you feel in need of suste-nance, then turning left soon leads to an excellent café run by the community in the large Glenelg & Arnisdale Community Hall.

Continue northwards round the coast on the Galltair road to another community

The Five Sisters of Kintail from Màm Ràtagan

The Cuillin Ridge from Elgol

run venture, the Glenelg-Skye ferry. The ferry boat, the Glenachulish, is the last manually operated turntable ferry in Scotland and a unique experience. There is a small charge for cyclists. As you cross you can try and imagine the drovers of old, swimming hundreds of cattle across the fast flowing strait.

Once on Skye, the climb up Kylerhea Glen to Bealach Udal is fairly gradual at first, before steepening (20%) just before the top, from where there are great views west to Broadford and the Red Cuillin. A lovely descent leads down Glen Arroch to the A87. Turn right and follow the A87 to the Skye Bridge

The ferry across Kyle Rhea

Elgol Extension
Once on Skye, continuing round the coast to Elgol, makes for a more challenging day; a GWR to a spectacular viewpoint overlooking the main Cuillin Ridge.
Where the descent from Bealach Udal meets the A87, turn left at the junction, head to Broadford and at the west end of the village, turn left onto the B8083 signposted to Elgol. This is fairly flat at the start then downhill as you make your way round Loch Slapin and underneath the brooding bulk of Blàbheinn. The route then climbs fairly steadily over the Strathaird peninsula, until you come to the final descent to Elgol. Enjoy the spectacular mountain views and the general goings on at the harbour until it is time to grovel your way back up the road (25%) under the watchful eyes of the café customers. If the weather is good the harbour can be very busy especially during July and August. The route is also worth doing if you just fancy something short and sweet – or should that be short and steep!
Distance 58km (36 miles); Height gain 600m (1969ft); Max gradient 25%; Approx time 2hrs 30mins

and Kyle of Lochalsh which has plenty of cafés and public toilets.

You could continue east on the A87 to Dornie, but that would mean missing out on another GWR. Just as you come into Kyle, take a left onto a minor road signposted to Plockton, which winds and weaves its way north round the coast.

Keep following the signs to Plockton, passing Erbusaig, Drumbuie and Duirinish to reach a T-junction. Turn left here signed to Plockton and cross the bridge over the Allt Dhuirinis. About 1km further on you descend a short hill to a junction at the bottom where you take a right, signposted to Stromeferry. (You can continue straight on for some 2km to the picturesque village of Plockton for tea and cakes if you wish, but you'll have to return to this junction.)

Go left at the next junction, signposted Stromeferry, and continue following the signs. As you head towards Stromeferry look out over Loch Carron to your left and you may see a thin sliver of a road slashing up through the hills of **Applecross** [29]; the Bealach na Bà, just waiting for you!

After 7km the road turns inland and leads to a junction just before Achmore where there is a bridge over a wooded river and a signpost pointing straight ahead to Stromeferry and Auchtertyre. Go right here onto a minor road, signposted to Braeintra, and climb gradually through mixed woodland to meet the A890, where you turn right.

A bit more of a climb, followed by a lovely sweeping descent with fine views, takes you down to the A87 where you turn left back to Dornie.

The mountains of Torridon across Upper Loch Torridon

North-east of Skye lie the wild lands of Wester Ross. This circuit goes through and over some of its most spectacular scenery and tackles, 'the toughest and wildest climb in Britain', the Bealach na Bà (pass of the cattle).

The road climbs from sea level to 626m then drops to sea level again and is one of the few roads in Britain which goes over the mountains rather than through them; quite a challenge. The only time I have seen this road busy is in August. A sportive tackles the challenge of this route in September – The Bealach Mòr.

I usually start at Achnasheen on the A832 and tackle the route in a clockwise direction. There is a car park at the railway station where you'll find toilets and a café. From here take the A890 south-west to Loch Carron and the sea. The road starts off wide and very open to the elements, but as you descend Glen Carron it becomes narrow and much more sheltered. At

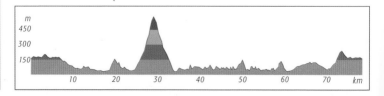

START & FINISH: *Achnasheen Railway Station (NH 163585)*

DISTANCE: *145km; 90 miles*

HEIGHT GAIN: *1800m; 5906ft*

MAX GRADIENT: *25%*

APPROX TIME: *7hrs*

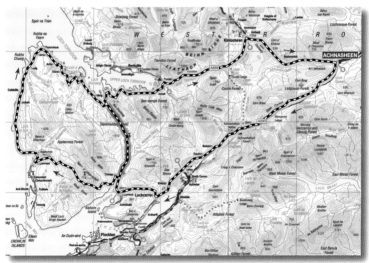

Liathach & Glen Torridon

the foot of the glen, continue ahead on the A896 and at the far end of Lochcarron village the road suddenly rears up (17%) and climbs up and over to Kishorn. It's just a wee warm up for what's to come!

As the road turns north up Loch Kishorn it flattens out and you come to a junction at Tornapress. Turn left onto the minor road, signposted to Applecross and the start of the climb up to the Bealach na Bà. It isn't that steep at first as it climbs above Loch Kishorn and ascends towards the impressive rock scenery of Sgùrr a' Chaorachain and The Cioch Nose, which lie straight ahead as you cross over the Russel Burn.

Just after this, the road swings left, then back right to reveal the Bealach na Bà, high in the distance. From here on the road steepens and doesn't really relent until the top. Just to make life more interesting there are some

sections of 25% at the hairpin bends below the bealach, but the road does level out a little in between – phew! Sections of crash barrier make it pretty hard for a climbing cyclist and a descending car to pass on this single track road, but most traffic is very sympathetic to sweaty cyclists grinding their way up.

Just a little bit further on from the last bend you reach the highest point with superb views of Skye, Raasay and Rona and, on a clear day, the Outer Hebrides. What a spot! Then there's a fine descent to Applecross, but take great care on the blind bends.

Just before the village is a sharp right-hand bend. Straight ahead leads to Applecross campsite and, more importantly, the Flower Tunnel café which is well worth a stop. Continuing right leads down to a T-junction in the village, where there are public toilets on the left. Turn right, signposted Shieldaig, and head round Applecross Bay, then climb northwards above the coast winding your way past rocky cliffs and sandy coves opposite Raasay and Rona. Be prepared for more short steep hills; it's another route that just keeps coming!

Fantastic views of the Torridon mountains greet you as the road rounds the tip of the peninsula to head south-east above Loch Torridon, before a final descent to the A896 and a left turn to Shieldaig. This pretty little village can be visited by a loop road which rejoins the main road further on. There is a shop and café in the village and public toilets at the campsite just off the main road.

There are a couple of short gradual climbs before reaching the flats of Upper Loch Torridon and the turn-off left to Torridon village. There are public toilets at the campsite to the left. Continue on the main road and a very gradual climb takes you through rugged Glen Torridon under the dominating bulk of Liathach.

Descend to Kinlochewe where there is a café and toilets, and turn right onto the A832. Unfortunately the climbing isn't over quite yet, although it's a fairly

> ### Glen Shieldaig Variation
> This is a good option to have in reserve if you don't fancy the climb over the Bealach na Bà and around the coast, or the weather looks doubtful. Going over the Bealach in bad weather can be an interesting experience. I have heard of people turning back having been blown over! At Tornapress, instead of turning left to Applecross and the Bealach na Bà, keep going north on the A896 through Glen Shieldaig to re-join the Applecross route just before Shieldaig.
> **Total distance 103km (64 miles); Height gain 640m (2100ft); Max gradient 17%; Approx time 4hrs**

gradual ascent up Glen Docherty to a height of 240m, followed by a descent to Loch a' Chroisg and back to Achnasheen.

A shorter circuit of the Applecross peninsula (71km; 44 miles) is also possible by starting at Tornapress or Shieldaig where there is adequate parking. This is the route of the Bealach Beag sportive, held in April or May.

The final bends below the Bealach na Bà

Approaching the Bealach na Bà

dramatic coastline,
combined with spectacular
and isolated mountains,
provides an impressive backdrop to this
circuit. It is described in some journals
as the 'most scenic road in Scotland'. It
certainly gets my vote as Number 1 in
the GWR hit parade.

This is a hilly route and the hills are at
their steepest (25%), when it is done
in a clockwise direction. The profile
looks like a saw blade and conse-
quently it has the lowest average speed

of any route in this guidebook. The
direction in which you do the circuit
will probably depend on which way the
wind is blowing. I have described it in
an anti-clockwise direction. There are
very few facilities along the way; cafés
and public toilets in Lochinver, a café in
Elphin and a shop in Drumbeg, but
that's about it.

Start about 15km north of Ullapool
on the A835, at a large layby on the
left, just before the scattered hosues of
Drumrunie and a single track road on

Beinn an Eoin & Ben More Coigach across Loch Bad a' Ghaill

the left, signposted to Achiltibuie. This minor road is followed on the return leg of the route.

From the layby continue north on the A835 climbing up and over to Elphin past the ancient schist rocks of the Moine Thrust at Knockan Crag. Turn left at the junction at Ledmore onto the A837, which leads to Loch Assynt and the ruins of Ardvreck Castle. Beyond

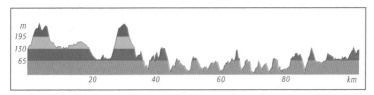

Heading towards Lochinver, with Suilven, Cul Mòr & Cul Beag in the distance

the castle ruin, turn right at Skiag Bridge onto the A894, signposted Kylesku, and start climbing to the col to the east of Quinag.

The mountain isn't very impressive from here, but things change on the descent and you can pretend you are sweeping down an alpine pass for a couple of minutes before turning left near the bottom onto the B869 single track road to Drumbeg and Lochinver.

This undulates along to Drumbeg so be prepared for quite a few 'undulations', some of which are quite steep

BEWARE
PIGS, PIGLETS
LAMBS, SHEEP
ON ROAD

(20%). Be careful on the descents as this is not a place to blow it. The scenery becomes more and more spectacular as you make your way west along the coast.

You'll pass a minor road signposted to Stoer which is a great place to come back to later for a walk out to the light-house and the 'Old Man', a spectacular sea-stack. Rejoin the A837 and turn right to Lochinver. At the south end of the village take a left turn signposted Inverkirkaig and Achiltibuie.

This soon becomes a single track road and the scenery keeps coming, as do the ups and downs, but they are never as steep as before. Eventually you descend to Loch Bad a' Ghaill, the solitary white house of Badnagyle, and a junction with the minor road out to Achiltibuie on the coast.

Turn left and enjoy the beautiful views of Ben More Coigach over to your right and Stac Pollaidh towering above the road, as you make your way beside Loch Lurgainn and, unfortunately, a final climb to the A835 at Drumrunie.

North to Suilven from Druim Bad a' Ghaill

mica *walkers' guides*

Available from high street and internet bookshops

www.micapublishing.com

60 walks
Loch Lomond and
The Trossachs
National Park
Vol 1 – West
by Tom Prentice

60 walks
Loch Lomond and The
Trossachs National
Park Vol 2 – East
by Tom Prentice

60 walks
The Pentland Hills
by Rab Anderson

60 walks
Lothian & Berwickshire
Coast
by Keith Fergus

60 walks
Scotland's Countryside
Parks Vol 1 – West
by Tom Prentice

60 walks
Scotland's Countryside
Parks Vol 2 –
Edinburgh & East
by Tom Prentice

60 walks
The Lakeland Fells
by Bernard Newman

Mica Publishing produces guidebooks to
the outdoors with an emphasis on wide
route choice, detailed coverage and high
photographic content